Circle of Sovereignty

CIRCLE of SOVEREIGNTY

PLOTTING POLITICS IN THE BOOK OF DANIEL

Danna Nolan Fewell

Abingdon Press
Nashville

CIRCLE OF SOVEREIGNTY:
PLOTTING POLITICS IN THE BOOK OF DANIEL

Library of Congress Cataloging-in-Publication Data

Fewell, Danna Nolan.

Circle of sovereignty: plotting politics on the book of Daniel / Danna Nolan Fewell. —2nd. rev. and extended ed.

p. cm.

Includes bibliographical references and indexes.

ISBN 0-687-08389-3

1. Bible. O.T. Daniel—Commentaries. 2. Politics in the Bible. I. Title.

BS155.3.F49 91-37195

224'.507—DC20 CIP

ISBN 0-687-08389-3

Printed in the United States of America
on recycled acid-free paper

To David

and the year of revisions

Who is like the sage?
And who knows the interpretation of a thing?

(Eccl. 8:1)

CONTENTS

PREFACE

In the first edition of this work (*Circle of Sovereignty: A Story of Stories in Daniel 1-6* [Sheffield: Almond, 1988]), a great deal of space was devoted to describing my method of reading. In the interim, literary critical work on biblical narrative has continued to flourish—so much so, that narrative criticism no longer needs to be explained in such detail. Discourses on the method (for example, Alter, Bar-Efrat, Berlin, Miscall, Sternberg, and Gunn and Fewell) are easily accessible to any reader who wishes to pursue narrative criticism's presuppositions, procedures, and interpretive possibilities.

Most narrative critics of the Bible start with the legacy of New Criticism, the close attention to language, structure, plot, characterization, point of view, thematic development. In recent years, however, critical emphasis has moved beyond the written text to include the reader. According to reader response theory, the reader, in the very act of reading the literary work, helps to *create the text.* Because different readers accent different elements, infer different meanings, sometimes literally see different things, texts are unstable, changing with each reading.

The focus on instability, called Deconstruction, is catching the interest of an increasing number of biblical critics. The idea that the meaning of a text cannot be finally determined can be frustrating, liberating, but at the very least fascinating. A text's multiple meanings are not always compatible; sometimes they are in tension with one another.

> It is this type of textual difference that informs the process of deconstructive criticism. *Deconstruction* is not synonymous with *destruction,* however. It is in fact much closer to the original meaning of the word *analysis,* which etymologically means "to undo"—a virtual synonym for "to de-construct." The de-construction of a text does not proceed

> by random doubt or arbitrary subversion, but by the careful teasing out of warring forces of signification within the text itself. If anything is destroyed in a deconstructive reading, it is not the text, but the claim to unequivocal domination of one mode of signifying over another . . . . (Johnson, 441)

Within a text, undercurrent meanings repeatedly disturb, if not displace, surface meanings. This reading of Daniel, admittedly, looks for undercurrents, meanings that subvert many of the traditional readings of the book.

This is not to say that my reading of Daniel is therefore necessarily "better" or "more correct" than other readings of Daniel. In many ways I am indebted to other readings, especially those produced by my colleagues in form criticism and folklore studies. In particular, the generic identifications made by scholars such as John Collins, Philip Davies, W. Lee Humphreys, Pamela Milne, Susan Niditch and Robert Doran have not only marked the typicalities of this material, but have pointed out the unusual features as well. Although they have focused on types, they have opened the door beyond. I have chosen to go through that door, playing with the notion that, while the material in Daniel shows affinities with other stories and visions, it has the capacity for depth and complexity.

Many people deserve my thanks. Sharyn Dowd, David Gunn, Lee Humphreys, Peter Miscall, and Carol Newsom have expressed their enthusiasm for the first edition of *Circle of Sovereignty*. I appreciate very much their (and their students') kind remarks and helpful suggestions.

As for the production of this second edition, I am indebted to the following people: To Rex Matthews of Abingdon Press for his eagerness to publish the work. To Gene Lovering of the Society of Biblical Literature who, with enviable expertise, performed some computer wizardry so that I could work with greater facility. To David Gunn of Columbia Theological Seminary who painstakingly edited the book and produced the camera-ready copy when he could have (and perhaps should have) been getting on with his own work.

—DANNA NOLAN FEWELL
PERKINS SCHOOL OF THEOLOGY

INTRODUCTION

A MATTER OF POLITICS

The political nature of the book of Daniel has long been recognized, especially by scholars who have explored its apocalyptic portions (essentially chapters 7-12). Having been written and circulated during a time of great political oppression, the apocalyptic visions of Daniel depict hierarchies of world power and political events both past and future. They seek to comfort marginalized Israelites caught in the middle of political tides beyond their control.

Most likely written and collected during a more peaceful but still difficult era, the stories (chapters 1-6), too, have manifested political dimensions. The stories, usually considered in service to the apocalyptic, are thought to contribute to a message of political passivity by showing how one can survive in the service of foreign power and still be faithful to one's beliefs. Furthermore, they reinforce the political authority of the visions in the latter half of the book by attributing them to a legendary hero known for his success and wisdom.

Despite the appeal of the apocalyptic to subsequent generations and the propensity of scholars in recent days to classify the entire book as an apocalypse, the book of Daniel introduces itself as narrative. An extended story comprised of six episodes about Daniel and his friends provides the literary context of the visions that follow. In the book's final form, the visions take their place among the events of the story world, events that are all, to some extent, political.

Like any other exegetical exercise, plotting the politics within the book of Daniel is not an objective endeavor. As reader and text intersect again and again, continuously raising questions for one another, patterns of meaning emerge. These patterns are sometimes dominant, sometimes subtle, sometimes incomplete. The initial question is mine: How do politics govern the plot and motivate the characters in the book of Daniel? As we examine the people and the events in the book, political concerns quickly converge with matters of religion, personal integrity, survival, success, and recognition to create complex, circular, and even subversive, messages.

The central political issue in Daniel is that of sovereignty. Who is sovereign in the human world? The question is, of course, also a theological one because the principal conflict in the book is between God and human monarchs over the very question: Who rules?

The question, as we shall see, is always pending in the story world because no solution is completely satisfactory. Real sovereignty, it seems, manifests itself in the control of human history, and history, as we all know, is a matter of time. As time progresses in the story, as events continue to happen, as different people take the stage, the question of who controls is voiced again and again. Every new cast of characters must learn the answer for itself.

The answer, however, refuses to be unequivocal. Sovereignty turns out to be a rather slippery beast that continues to elude all contenders. An unsettled question results in an unfinished story. Each narrative episode, each vision tries, unsuccessfully, to bring closure to the subject, but sovereignty merely makes another turn.

Where does that leave the readers of Daniel? Like Daniel himself, we are left waiting for an end that does not come, watching sovereignty slide back and forth between the human and the divine. A reason for despair? Perhaps for some. But others may find meaning in the circle, for in God's endurance, we can hope for our own.

Chapter One

DANIEL 1

EATING FROM THE KING'S HAND

Two Sovereigns: Verses 1-2

The book of Daniel begins with an ending.

> In the third year of the reign of Jehoiakim king of Judah, Nebuchadnezzar king of Babylon came to Jerusalem and besieged it. Adonai gave Jehoiakim king of Judah into his hand along with some of the vessels of the house of God. He brought them to the land of Shinar, to the house of his god, and he placed the vessels in the treasury of his god. (1:1-2)

Nebuchadnezzar's capture of Jerusalem, the royal family, and the vessels from the house of God ends a story of life in the Judean homeland. The ending of the old story provides the setting for the new and, though the new story takes over, it is curiously subordinated to the old. Rather than offering a reference point in the new story world, "In such-and-such year of Nebuchadnezzar, king of Babylon," the narrator invokes instead the time line of the old story world: "In the third year of the reign of Jehoiakim[1] king of Judah." In order to appreciate the ensuing story, that seems to say, one must know something of the story that precedes.

The old story world sets the new story world in relief. Homeland gives way to alien land. At least a similitude of political autonomy turns into political captivity. A native, though weak, king is harshly succeeded by a strong, but foreign, one.

Daniel 1 is both a story and an exposition to a larger story, in the first instance the narrative of Daniel 1-6 and, conceived more broadly, the entire book of Daniel. Consequently, the ending that begins Daniel 1 (1:1-2) is strategic not only for the first short story, but also for the story that continues beyond chapter 1. Besides locating small and large story alike in time and place, it introduces a dramatic irony that permeates both the first story and the conflict that is to develop through the ensuing chapters.

The dramatic irony is the product of two disparate points of view. First, there is the perspective of Nebuchadnezzar, king of Babylon. As far as he is concerned, the conflict reported in verses 1-2 primarily involves himself and Jehoiakim king of Judah. His conquest of Jerusalem is, he believes, the result of his own action. He *comes* (*bôʾ*), he *besieges*, he *takes* (*bôʾ*), he *places* (*bôʾ*). After victory he acknowledges the help of his god. His transfer of the temple vessels from Jerusalem to the treasury of his god in Shinar, suggests that, in Nebuchadnezzar's point of view, the human conflict mirrors a divine conflict. His god has defeated the god of Jerusalem. In short, Nebuchadnezzar sees himself and the god of Babylon as victors over Jehoiakim and the god of Jerusalem.

Though for the narrator the outcome of these events is the same, their cause is quite a different matter. Nebuchadnezzar does not defeat Jehoiakim through his own skill or power. His image of himself as a successful aggressor is overshadowed by the narrator's view that the Babylonian king is but a passive recipient: *Adonai gives* Jehoiakim into Nebuchadnezzar's hand. Thus the narrator and the reader know something that the king does not.

The narrator's point of view realigns the characters, creating a dynamic in the first story that becomes even more prominent in the succeeding episodes. According to the narrator, the issue is not between Nebuchadnezzar and his god, on the one hand, and Jehoiakim and his god, on the other. Two of these four parties, namely Jehoiakim and Nebuchadnezzar's god, quickly fade into the background and, essentially, die to the story. Nebuchadnezzar and the narrator's god ("narrator's god" because, through the choice of *Adonai*, "my lord," the narrator confesses allegiance) emerge as the only two characters to survive the exposition. Their relationship is curiously conflicted. On the one hand, Adonai and Nebuchadnezzar are allies. They have both sought the same thing—the defeat of Jerusalem. On the other hand, Nebuchadnezzar does not recognize Adonai as the source of his victory. He does not know this god and he offers this god no credit. Thus the potential conflict is born.

By pairing Adonai's will with Nebuchadnezzar's activity, the narrator braces the story with a certain theological worldview. First of all, appeal to Adonai's will explains the theological difficulty of the conquest of Jerusalem and the temple's destruction. Secondly, by attributing the exile to Adonai, the narrator constructs a world in which Adonai is in control of events and capable of manipulating foreign rulers, even unbelievers. Thirdly, with the idea that Adonai has turned against Judah, the narrator implies that the people have done something to cause their god to be angry. Though the reason for the anger is unspecified, its justification is unquestioned. Commonly in Israelite literature, that is, in the "old story," God's anger against the Israelites is caused by their religious or political apostasy. Whether readers will supply such motivation here, fill this gap this way, depends upon their familiarity with the story's larger context. Finally, Adonai may be a punisher in the worldview of the story in Daniel 1, but Adonai is also a protector. God's participation in the fall of Jerusalem, the end of the older story, foreshadows the possibility of God's participation in the story about to be told. The possibilities of hope and despondency are raised and held in tension.

The Rite of Passage: Verses 3-7

The story continues with Nebuchadnezzar's perspective. He is in control. He wastes no time in making the most of his victory. He commands his chief eunuch, Ashpenaz, to select some of the captives for royal service. Those to be chosen can be nothing but the very best—best by blood, best of appearance, best in intelligence. Nebuchadnezzar insists that the captive young nobles be "without blemish." To be without blemish in service of sovereignty—can the reader not hear an echo from the older story? Yahweh requires sacrifices and those in divine service to be without blemish (Lev 22:17-25; 21:16-24).[2] Allusion subliminally pairs the two sovereigns, pitting them one against the other as they vie for the allegiance of their subjects.

The selected captives are to undergo a period of training in which they are "to learn the letters and language of the Chaldeans" and so ready themselves for service in the Babylonian court. The stage is set for a success story like that of Joseph or Esther (where the chosen women also undergo extensive preparation): Jewish captive makes good, or something of the sort. The reader might even be tempted to consider Nebuchadnezzar a generous, tolerant monarch with worthy aesthetic and intellectual values.

Nevertheless, even if success lies ahead, our reading of Daniel 1 could use some subtle shading. The situation of the captives in their captor's plans is highly ambiguous and loaded with tension. Backtrack but a moment and a reader will recall which captives the king singles out: young men from the "royal seed" and from the nobility. The royalty and the nobility are those who have the greatest stake in political autonomy. Is it not a tricky business to transform former enemies into trustworthy courtiers?

What, exactly, is involved in this training process? First, the young men are to "learn the letters and language of the Chaldeans." The term Chaldeans is an ambiguous one in the story world of Daniel. It is, on the one hand, the designation of a class of professional sages (cf. Dan 2:2-10; 3:8-12; 4:7; 5:7). Thus, "the letters and language of the Chaldeans" could refer to a field of knowledge. On the other hand, Chaldean is also used as an ethnic label (cf. Dan 5:30; also 9:1). In that case the reader may associate the learning of Chaldean language and literature with instruction in Chaldean culture. Consequently, the choice of the term "Chaldean" rather than "sage" or "magician" suggests that the training involves national (and thus political) as well as professional indoctrination.

Besides providing guidelines for the captives' education, the king also stipulates their diet, assigning food and wine from his own table. His prescription follows from his insistence upon physical perfection (vs. 4). But this diet also has political connotations. The rebellion against the king of the south in Dan 11:26 is unexpected and extreme because the rebels eat the king's *patbag*; they eat from the king's table (cf. Baldwin, 82-83). We know from the older story, of life in the land, that eating from the king's table symbolizes political covenant and compromise. When David stops eating at Saul's table, Saul surmises that David has rebelled against him (1 Sam 20:30-34). Perhaps to keep his claim to the throne secure, King David demands that the last remaining member of Saul's family, Mephibosheth, eat (always) at the king's table (2 Sam 9:9-13). Jehoiachin, after the fall of Judah, spends his last days in captivity, eating from the Babylonian king's table

(2 Kgs 25:27-29). Given this pattern, it is reasonable to suppose that, by assigning such a diet, Nebuchadnezzar is imposing political allegiance. The captives are to depend upon him and be indebted to him for their very existence, not to mention their social success.

The king gives them three years to complete their development before standing in attendance at court. Their development is to be both physical and mental as the diet and education make clear. To stand before the king, they are to be physically perfect, mentally astute, culturally sophisticated, and, as advisors, politically loyal.

After relating the king's intentions, the narrator narrows the reader's vision from the general group to four specific captives (vss. 6-7). Among the Judeans, the narrator tells us, are Daniel, Hananiah, Mishael, and Azariah. When the chief eunuch takes charge of the young men, he assigns them Babylonian names: Belteshazzar, Shadrach, Meshach, and Abednego.[3]

What is being forced upon the young men here fits the classic model of a *rite of passage*, a ritual designed to facilitate a person's passing from one phase of life into another (van Gennep 1960; Turner 1967, 1969, 1974). Initiates participating in a rite of passage go through three basic stages in the ritual process. First, they are separated from their community and put in seclusion (so Nebuchadnezzar's first command in vs. 3). Once secluded from normal society, they endure a temporary "betwixt and between" or "liminal" existence in which they are taught special knowledge that will enable them to function in their new roles ("the letters and language of the Chaldeans"). They are fed special food (the king's *patbag* and wine). Instructors—to whom they must be completely submissive—encourage the initiates to suppress their former allegiances (for example, attachments to mother or father, but here, political allegiance to Judah's royal house) and elevate their new allegiances (for example, to husband or wife, but here, to Nebuchadnezzar, king of Babylon). These induced experiences in the liminal stage are designed to bring about a change of being, a change of identity (and thus, the symbolic renaming). The third stage of the process is reintegration into society. (Our narrator alludes to this step in verse 5 and reports it explicitly in verse 18.)

This match between Nebuchadnezzar's plans and a rite of passage strengthens our understanding of the training as not simply professional education. The young men are to learn the Babylonian way of life, adopt a Babylonian profession, and confess Babylonian allegiance.

Such a transformation benefits the king; the captives must be made to see that such a transformation benefits them as well. The narrator, however, leaves the reader two options for judging what is happening to the young Judeans. In one sense their rite of passage is a promotion from prisoners to professionals. But in another sense, the passage is a demotion from "royal seed" to servanthood.

Daniel's Resolution: Verses 8-16

To all of this activity the prisoners make no response. Their point of view is not reported. They are as faceless and voiceless as Jehoiakim the defeated king. The narrator, however, narrows our vision further.

> Daniel resolved that he would not defile himself with the king's special food or with the wine which he drank. And so he requested of the chief eunuch that he not have to defile himself. (1:8)

One character, Daniel, begins to awaken to the story. Precisely at the point of renaming, the pace of the narration slows and we see the effect of the plan and Daniel's response. After the chief eunuch "fixes upon" or "sets for" them (*yasem*) Babylonian names, Daniel "fixes" or "sets" (*yasem*) upon his heart that he will not defile himself with the king's food or drink.

The narrator's internal view of Daniel as he makes his silent decision does not clarify what prompts Daniel's resolve or why he thinks the king's food and drink would be defiling. However, by making the shift of perspective pivot on the verb "to set or fix," the narrator suggests that the assignment of new identity may be part of what spurs Daniel to show resistance. In other words, Daniel is attempting to limit in some way the all-consuming process of indoctrination.

The term *ga'al*, to defile, also offers a clue to Daniel's motivation.[4] Since (at least in this late spelling) *ga'al* is normally used to refer to cultic pollution, the word invites the reader to understand Daniel's aversion to the food to be motivated by religious piety. By introducing the idea of defilement, the narrator permits the speculation that the assigned food and drink are not in accordance with Israel's dietary laws and are, consequently, ritually polluting.[5]

There are problems, however, with this understanding of the defilement as specifically cultic. In the first place, the narrator implies that Daniel makes his decision concerning the food before it is ever actually presented to him. He does not know what the king's *patbag* includes; he only knows that the king has assigned it. An aversion to the food on ritual grounds might be feasible in terms of meat, because of its kind (Lev 3:17; 11:1-47) or method of preparation (Lev 17:10-14), but his refusal of the wine makes no sense at all if Levitical law is the assumed dietary guide. In a reading of the book's final form, moreover, Dan 10:3 implies either that Daniel does not view meat and wine (also labeled desirable or delightful food) *per se* to be a problem of cultic defilement or that Daniel, in his later years, drastically relaxes his religious principles concerning diet. Furthermore, the defiling nature of food eaten in exile could be argued to be unavoidable (cf. Ezek 4:13; Hos 9:3, 4). In other words, choosing not to be ritually defiled by food is not an option for captives (Baldwin, 83).

It is not simply a matter of the food and wine being, in themselves, defiling. Rather, Daniel's rejection of the diet has more to do with the food's *source*. It is the *king's* special food and the wine which the *king* himself drinks. And, as Philip Davies (1985:90-91) has well observed, there are political dimensions to the king's food. The food and wine are, in other words, the symbols of political patronage; to consume them would be tantamount to declaring complete political allegiance.

This interpretation of Daniel's action does not deny his religious motivation; it suggests rather that his religiosity is complex. His piety extends beyond cultic or ritual concerns. We are given no indication that Daniel is aware that it is Adonai who has given Jerusalem's royalty and holy things to Nebuchadnezzar. How can he in good conscience confess unqualified allegiance to the man who he believes is responsible for destroying and plundering the temple of his god? Daniel's mixture of religious and political interests is understandable. Daniel is, after all, at least a Judean noble if not a member of Judah's royal family (a descendent of Zedekiah, according to Josephus, *Antiquities* 10.10.1). Though his discrete gesture of resistance may amount to little in the course of political history (that is, the political history of the story world), it is an attempt to express some modicum of personal control in a seemingly uncontrollable situation.[6]

When Daniel asks the chief eunuch that he not have to defile himself, the narrator tells us that Elohim gives Daniel favor and compassion before the officer (vs. 9). The chief eunuch is sympathetic, but realistic. The gist of his response is a simple pragmatic refusal. For the reader, however, his words may conjure more complexity, continuing to blend religion and politics.

"I fear my lord the king who appointed your food and drink," he begins (vs. 10). The apellative "my lord," *adoni*, echoes the narrator's use of Adonai earlier in the story. Each occurrence reflects the speaker's sense of hierarchy and allegiance. For the chief eunuch, lordship belongs to the king; for the narrator, lordship belongs to God. The use of *adoni/Adonai*, then, reflects the crux of Daniel's dilemma—the acknowledgment of sovereignty.

The speech continues ambiguously: "If he [the king] should view *penekem zo‘aphim* in comparison to the young men around you, you would bring guilt upon my head before the king." *Penekem zo‘aphim* can be translated variously. It can be taken to reflect the chief eunuch's view of the relationship between the food and a healthy appearance: "If he should view your appearance [or condition] to be inferior [or poorer] in comparison to the other young men." On the other hand, "face" can refer to a person's expression as well as appearance (cf. 3:19), and *za‘aph* literally means to be displeased, even angry. Consequently, the answer, while giving Daniel's request the benefit of the doubt, takes into account political ramifications: "I fear my lord the king . . . should view your expressions to be discontent [or even malcontent?] in comparison with the young men around you and you would bring guilt upon my head before the king." This language mixes the issue of healthy appearance with the issue of attitude. Refusing the king's food symbolizes political dissent and, in the opinion of the eunuch, such an attitude will eventually become more obvious. The official will take no responsibility for nonconformity.

Daniel, nevertheless, refuses to give up. Inspired by the wordplay on healthy appearance, he tries a new tactic. Going behind the chief eunuch's back (cf. Montgomery, 134), he solicits help from his own special guardian. Making clear that his friends are also involved, he proposes a conditional program:

> "Please test your servants for ten days. Let us be given vegetables to eat and water to drink. Then observe our appearance and the appearances of the young men who have eaten the king's *patbag* and, according to what you observe, so deal with your servants." (1:12-13)

This request is quite different from his previous appeal to the chief eunuch. He says nothing here about defilement; in fact, he gives the guardian no reason at all for the change of menu. He proposes the idea simply as a "test," stipulates a limited period of time, and so minimizes any risk on the guardian's part. His cleverest tactic, however, is to portray the situation exclusively in physical terms. He carefully uses the term "appearance" (*mar'eh*), referring to a person's physical appearance as viewed by someone else, rather than the ambiguous "face" (*peni*) which could also connote expression or demeanor. He omits the chief eunuch's concern about *za'aph*, discontent. He allows the guardian to think that all he need worry about is whether or not the four captives look healthy. The proposal is sweetened also by what is unspoken—the guardian is left to dispose of the king's food and wine (surely much better fare than that to which the guardian is accustomed) as he sees fit! Small wonder that the request is granted.

After ten days, Daniel and his friends look better and healthier than the other young men (vs. 16), though the narrator never explains the exact relationship between the different food and their superior appearances. Thus the situation continues (vs. 17), with everyone involved all the happier with the agreement. Daniel and his friends can discretely confess allegiance to a higher authority and so preserve themselves from being completely consumed into Babylonian life. And as for the guardian, he is quite content to "take" their food and wine.

God's Gift:
Verses 17-21

The narrative tempo now picks up considerably. The remainder of the three years of training is covered as the narrator describes the success of Daniel and his friends:

> As for these four young men, Elohim gave them knowledge and made them skilful in all letters and wisdom and, as for Daniel, he understood all dreams and visions. (1:17)

All of them excel in wisdom and knowledge, but Daniel is singled out as having an additional talent regarding dreams and visions.[7] The reader is thus prepared for Daniel's prominence in the rest of the book and in particular for his distinctive role as interpreter of mysteries.

According to the narrator, the superior skills of these four young men are not due to their fine Babylonian education but to Elohim's graciousness. Indeed, the only verb associated with God in Daniel 1 is the verb "give." Adonai gives Jehoiakim and the temple vessels to Nebuchadnezzar (vs. 2). Elohim gives Daniel *ḥesed* and compassion during his interview with the chief eunuch (vs. 9). Elohim gives the four young men unsurpassed wisdom and knowledge (vs. 17). By revealing God's participation in the story, the narrator lets the reader in on a secret concealed from some if not from all of the characters. What the Babylonians think to be the result of their own effort is, in actuality, the result of God's intervention. As far as the four young Judeans are concerned, the narrator leaves uncertain the extent to which they recognize their skills to be gifts from God.

The training ended, the young men are brought to the king; and "none among them were found to be like Daniel, Hananiah, Mishael, and Azariah. They stood in attendance before the king" (vs. 19).

Irony of ironies! The four who disobey the king's orders are the four who show themselves to be exceptional. The four who refuse to align themselves politically with the king are the ones chosen for royal service. Underscoring their independence, the narrator uses their Hebrew names rather than their assigned Babylonian names. Thus, though they stand in royal service, they are not what they seem, in the king's eyes, to be. The illusion of political unanimity covers the reality of compromise and raises a question for the reader: What will happen later, in the larger story, if these men are called upon to prove their political fidelity?

The story ends with a coda that closes the story's temporal frame and brings the reader out of the story's time:

> In every matter of wisdom and understanding about which the king questioned them, he found them ten times better than all the magicians and enchanters who were in all his kingdom. So it was with Daniel until the first year of Cyrus the king. (1:20-21)

For the remainder of their service, the four Judeans continue to surpass their peers to a degree that later makes them targets of conspiracy. As for Daniel in particular, his career spans the exile itself. He is the link between the beginning and the end, between Nebuchadnezzar and Cyrus, between destruction and restoration. The narrator jumps to the end of the exilic story to tell us of Daniel's success and thereby captures our curiosity. What happens to Daniel, we want to know, in the meantime, between here and there, between now and then?

Chapter Two

DANIEL 2

SUCH DREAMS AS KINGS ARE MADE OF

In the Second Year of Nebuchadnezzar: Verse 1

In the second year of his reign, Nebuchadnezzar has a dream that leaves him troubled (vs. 1). Here in a single sentence we have the exposition to chapter 2, the introduction that establishes the time and initial situation of the story. This dream sets the story in motion and becomes the focal interest of narrator, characters and readers alike.

"The second year of Nebuchadnezzar" both orients and disorients the reader. On the one hand, it informs us that Nebuchadnezzar is relatively new to the throne. Perhaps, then, the king's restless and troubled sleep stems from political insecurity (cf. Baldwin, 85-86, 92). On the other hand, when read in the context of Daniel 1 which spanned three years, this temporal designation suggests that we are dealing with a flashback. The reader must suppose that, in the chronology of the story world of Daniel 1-6, Nebuchadnezzar captures Jerusalem in his first year and dreams unsettling dreams in his second.[1]

This opening sentence, read thus, shows another side of Nebuchadnezzar. The self-confident military aggressor (that is, the king's self-perception in chapter 1) is a less confident administrator, now that the days of military glory are over. Could it be that Nebuchadnezzar finds *retaining* control decidedly more difficult than *taking* control?

The exposition focuses immediate attention upon the king, but it also carries over from chapter 1 the reader's interest in Daniel. With the mention of the dream, we are reminded of Daniel's special talent, understanding in all dreams and visions. If the conflict in the plot now is going to revolve around a problematic dream, we expect that Daniel will have something to do with any resolution.

Tell the Dream!
Verses 2-12

Troubled by his dream, the king summons his professional sages (vs. 2). And so we enter the story's first major scene. The list of specialized personnel—magicians, conjurers, sorcerers, and Chaldeans—suggests that the brightest and best Babylonian scholars are represented. (If one reads chapter 2 as a flashback, Daniel's absence from this interview finds a ready explanation—he is still undergoing initiation.)

The narrator makes a point of explaining to the audience that the sages are called before the king "in order to tell the king his dreams." A seemingly innocent statement, it appears to be ambiguous. Expectation (cf. Joseph in Genesis 41) may lead a reader to interpret this phrase to mean something like "in order to help the king understand his dream(s)." In reality, however, the statement is neither innocent nor ambiguous. It is quite literal and it foreshadows the coming complication. The *telling* of the dream itself, and not simply the interpreting of the dream, is a critical part of the king's agenda.

The scene involving the sages before their sovereign (vss. 2-12) is structured by the popular storytelling device of trebling. Three times the king makes his request to the sages; three times they answer. With each interchange, the tension mounts.

In his opening words (vs. 3) the king tells the sages of the event that the narrator has just reported to the reader. "I have dreamed a dream," he says, adding an implicit request, "and my spirit is troubled to know the dream." The sages misunderstand, thinking that the king merely wants them to interpret his dream. As a collective character, they respond in unison and with confidence, "Tell the dream to your servants and we will disclose the interpretation" (vs. 4).

Irritated, the king in turn misunderstands. As his next words indicate, he seems to think that they understand the request, but are avoiding it. Hence he issues them an ultimatum: "If you do not make known to me the dream and its interpretation, you will be dismembered and your houses will be laid in ruins. But if you do disclose the dream and its interpretation, you will receive gifts, rewards, and great honor from me" (vss. 5-6). He finishes with a command: "Therefore, disclose to me the dream and its interpretation!" At this point perhaps it begins to dawn on the sages that the king is actually commanding them to recount the dream itself. They are caught off guard and cannot think of anything else to say. They feebly repeat their first response (though in a more respectful tone) as if to give the king the benefit of the doubt, "Let the king tell [compare the imperative 'tell' in vs. 4] the dream to his servants that we might disclose the interpretation" (vs. 7).

With the king's third speech, however, their worst fears are confirmed. The king accuses them of evading the issue and of conspiring to deceive him. He throws back in their faces their own first words: "Tell me the dream so that I will know that you can disclose to me its interpretation" (vs. 9; cf. vs. 4). The sages explain to the king that they cannot do what the king has asked because the task does not fall within the range of human capabilities. Such a request has no historical precedent. Only a deity could do such a thing (vss. 10-11).

Here the dialogue ends. The king loses his temper completely and orders that all the sages of Babylon are to be executed (vs. 12). The scene is over. The sages have been dismissed—ultimately.

In this first scene the narrator tells us *what* happens but not *why* it happens. Why does the king want the dream told? Two mutually exclusive explanations could be offered.

Let us suppose that he has forgotten the dream, suppressing some unpleasantry, perhaps. "I am troubled to know the dream" would then be a literal confession and his irrational demand to be told the dream a result of his frustrating inability to remember. A sense of foreboding which he could not articulate would then lead to his unmitigated anger (cf. Baldwin, 87-88; Lacocque, 38).

The alternative supposition is that he has not forgotten the dream, but for some reason feels the need to test the ability of his sages (cf. Bentzen, 225). If they can tell the dream, then he can trust their interpretation. Perhaps political anxiety has produced suspicion of his royal advisors. Thus, the accusation, "You have conspired to speak a false and corrupt word before me until the present situation [literally, the time] is changed," can be read as an expression of the king's insecurity, his paranoia that his courtiers are awaiting the downfall of his reign. Or perhaps Nebuchadnezzar's decision to test the sages is arbitrary and we are being led to interpret his unreasonable demand as a sign of a dangerous, unpredictable, even sadistic character.

By not reporting the content of the dream at the point in which Nebuchadnezzar dreams it, the narrator steers the reader's sympathy toward the sages. Like them, we have no idea what the king has dreamed. Our lack of knowledge aligns our view with their view that, indeed, the king's request is absurd.

The King's Sentence: Verses 13-16

Verse 13 makes a transition into the story's next movement. The sentence of execution is promulgated, the narrator informs us, and Daniel and his friends are among those to be executed. Clearly the way this information is presented implies a reader familiar with Daniel and his friends. These characters are given no introduction; they are not described or identified. Simply their involvement is noted. That fits with a narrator who assumes that the reader can supply and flesh out the characters' identity from what has already been recounted (in chapter 1). Thus this way of indicating the characters' involvement confirms our reading of a story within a story and not (as the form critics would have it) a discrete tale. Indeed, this information about the friends reinforces the interest that the subject of the dream may have stirred. If that subject, also reaching back into chapter 1, led us to expect that Daniel might be participating in this story, then we were correct. Thus in their present form, the stories in chapters 1 and 2 flow into each other.

The narrator's manipulation of our interest in Daniel, the Judean exile, suggests that the implied reader of this second chapter, too, is one who has, at the least, knowledge of and, at the most, a stake in the larger story of Israel. In other words, the implied reader is to be located somewhere in the matrix of Judeo-Christian traditions. Up until this point, the reader might only be mildly concerned with the fate of Babylonian sages. But once Daniel and his friends are included in the crisis, the reader's involvement in (and enjoyment of) the story intensifies.

Given chapter 1, the king's sentence becomes all the more monstrous. Not only is he willing to kill all the fully fledged sages for the failure of a few to accomplish the impossible, but his order extends even to those who are merely preparing to become his future advisors. Yet if we continue to read his character as motivated by political insecurity, then his move to purge his advisory staff (even those in training), though an extreme gesture, makes some perverse sense. After all, those in training are from the royal and noble seed of a conquered nation. Perhaps his present courtiers are from similar stock. Any of them could have political designs of their own.

The narrator now shifts our attention to a different location and to different characters (vss. 14-24). The executioner is the transitional figure who takes us from the presence of the king to an encounter with Daniel in an unidentified location. The executioner, who has both name, Arioch, and title, captain of the royal guard, is the one who is to mediate the king's sentence against the sages. On the mechanical level of the plot, he is an agent who mediates knowledge as well. If Daniel is to resolve the conflict, and thus fulfill our expectations, then Daniel must find out what has transpired. Arioch is the informant who insures the continuation of the plot.

In terms of the story's mechanics, Arioch is, like the chief eunuch and the guardian in chapter 1, basically a functional character. But, in terms of the story's social world, he is, also like the eunuch and the guardian, a character with power and authority. Daniel, whose wisdom obviously includes the art of diplomacy, wins the man's confidence. He tactfully questions Arioch concerning the sentence of execution. Arioch, who perhaps has yet to begin the massacre and who seems not overly eager to fulfill his task, explains the matter to Daniel and allows him to ask for royal reprieve.[2] Somewhat surprisingly, the reprieve is implicitly granted. It seems that, for whatever reason, Daniel is allowed to "buy time" that was not afforded to the earlier group of sages, even though he, at this point, has no answer either. The execution is postponed.

Daniel's Vision:
Verses 17-23

In the next scene (vss. 17-23), Daniel leaves the company of Arioch and returns to his house. He tells his companions what is happening and they petition the God of heaven. According to the narrator, Daniel seeks divine compassion "so that Daniel and his friends would not be destroyed with the rest of the sages of Babylon" (vs. 18). Notice what the wording is not. It could have been "so that Daniel, his friends, *and the rest of the sages of Babylon* would not be destroyed." Daniel's primary motivation is self-preservation and the preservation of his friends. Only secondarily is he concerned with his professional colleagues who are, in the scheme of things, also Daniel's potential rivals.

The mystery is revealed to Daniel in a vision during the night. Here, as at the beginning, is a prime opportunity to present the content of the dream, but again, the narrator refrains from disclosure. Told that Daniel now has the answer, the reader's sense of suspense is likely to decrease substantially. Although we do not know precisely what form a resolution will take, we can be confident that Daniel will indeed prove himself capable of fulfilling the king's demand. Nevertheless, our interest may remain captive on account of our curiosity concerning what is now past. We wait to learn the content of Daniel's vision, which is, for the most part, the content of Nebuchadnezzar's dream. Of course, some degree of suspense is retained through what we have seen of Nebuchadnezzar's volatile character. The dream, after all, was a troubling dream. The revelation of its meaning has the potential for disaster.

This episode at night in Daniel's house (vss. 17-23) contains critical elements that make the story unique among tales of a similar type. The act of prayer, the answer to prayer, and the presence of the divine helper are, Susan Niditch and Robert Doran argue (190), the motifs that turn the story's focus from human wisdom, the usual focus of such a tale, to divine revelation. Indeed, we can agree that in this pivotal scene, divine revelation does emerge as a prominent theme, but not without ambiguity. It is, as its image portrays, a vision that comes in darkness.

This scene makes the point foreshadowed earlier by the sages (vs. 11) that only a god has the ability to do what the king has asked. But as we examine the scene more closely, we soon discover that divine ability is rather difficult to distinguish from human ability. Daniel does "seek compassion from *before the God of heaven*" and he does learn the mystery that he later reports *before the king*. But, rather than stating, as we might have expected, that "*God* revealed the mystery to Daniel," the narrator reports the event in passive voice, "the mystery was revealed to Daniel." The narrator does not allow the "divine helper" to be a character. God does nothing that we can see. God says nothing that we can hear.

We are forced to depend upon human revelation to learn anything of divine revelation. We must trust Daniel's song of thanksgiving (vss. 20-23) for information about God's role in the story. Daniel praises God for being the source of wisdom and for being the controller of natural and political history. In praising God's wisdom he is responding to the revelatory event of his vision. His words verify that God is the vision's source. On the one hand, his affirmation is like that of the sages: The divine can reveal what human beings cannot. On the other hand, his affirmation stands in contrast to the sages' view that gods "do not dwell with the flesh." Not only does he portray God as involved in human affairs, but he also claims that divine wisdom and strength (intellectual strength, perhaps) can be given to humans, and in fact, *has* been given to him. Divine wisdom can only be recognized and praised when it is revealed to human beings and, once human beings have obtained divine wisdom, it loses its quality of "otherness." The pious language that elevates divine transcendence also, ironically, minimizes divine transcendence. Divine wisdom is "knowable." By the end of his response, the "God of heaven" has become the "God of my fathers."

Daniel Before the King: Verses 24-30

After Daniel learns the mystery, he goes to Arioch and instructs him, "Do not destroy the sages of Babylon. Bring me before the king and I will disclose the interpretation . . ." (vs. 24). He does not say "I will disclose what God has revealed to me." At least to Arioch, Daniel makes no distinction between his ability and God's revelation.

This brief scene with Arioch mirrors the earlier one involving these two characters (vss. 14-15) and closes the frame surrounding the nocturnal vision. In the earlier scene with Arioch, the execution procedures are instigated; in the latter the execution procedures are halted. In the earlier scene Arioch informs Daniel of the problem; in the latter scene Daniel informs Arioch that he has the solution.

Verse 24 also initiates a transition into the final major movement of the story. The instrumental nature of Arioch's role makes the transition work. Just as he brings the problem of the story to Daniel's attention in verse 15, an action which is necessary for the development of the plot, likewise he brings Daniel to the attention of the king, thereby facilitating the resolution of the story.

In verse 25 Arioch "hastily" takes Daniel before the king and introduces him. Arioch's reason for haste is left to speculation. Is he concerned for the king in his dilemma? Is he worried about the lives of the sages? Is he anxious to gain personal recognition? In his announcement to the king, he echoes Daniel's use of the first person pronoun and takes credit for himself: "*I* have found a man among the Judean exiles who can make the interpretation known to the king" (cf. Baldwin, 91). However, if reward is what he seeks, he is to be disappointed. The king immediately turns his attention to Daniel and Arioch is not mentioned again.

This scene at the king's court is built around the king's point of view so that, to some extent, the reader's point of view is channeled through that of the king. Daniel is introduced to Nebuchadnezzar, not by his Hebrew name, but as the king perceives him, "a man from among the Judean exiles." As far as the king is concerned, Daniel's name is Belteshazzar (vs. 26). (The use of the name Belteshazzar gives further support to reading Daniel 2 as a flashback. Daniel has been in training long enough to receive a new name, but he has not been formally introduced to the king's court.) The king's address to Belteshazzar qualifies Arioch's exclusive mention of the interpretation; he is concerned that the young sage before him be able "to make known *the dream*" as well as its interpretation.

As Daniel responds, the reader hears what Nebuchadnezzar hears. Like the king, we wait to hear the dream come from Daniel's lips, but, like the king we must first listen to Daniel's rather verbose preamble. He explains how he came to know the dream and of the significance of the king's having such a dream to begin with.

Daniel's introductory remarks are packed with irony. He first, indirectly and perhaps unintentionally, defends the sages who have failed to fulfill the king's demand. He reiterates what the sages themselves have said earlier (vss. 10-11), that no one, not even a professional sage, is capable of making such a mystery known. Having said this, he goes on to talk about a god in heaven who reveals mysteries and who, Daniel purports to know, has revealed to Nebuchadnezzar, through the dream, the mystery of the future (vs. 28). He begins to tell about the dream by describing its circumstances: "While you were upon your bed, O King, your thoughts arose of what is to be after this" (vs. 29). Then, as if realizing that he has not clarified how he himself knows the dream—especially since he has so boldly claimed that no human could know such a thing—he interrupts his narration with a rather awkward disclaimer: "But as for me, it is not because there is more wisdom in me than in all else living that this mystery was revealed to me, but it was in order that the interpretation could be made known to the king and you could know your innermost thoughts" (vs. 30).

Revelation occurs for the king's sake. Certainly this is a reason designed to appease the king. But does Daniel really know God's reason for revealing the mystery to him? Or do we, for that matter? (We were never allowed to hear God speak.) All we know is why Daniel asked that the mystery be revealed and, at the time, that reason had nothing to do with the king's knowing his own innermost thoughts. Daniel, it will be recalled, "sought compassion before the God of heaven concerning this mystery so that Daniel and his friends *would not be destroyed* . . ." (vs. 18).

Moreover, does Daniel really believe that his own wisdom has nothing to do with God's revelation? In his song he said, "[God] gives wisdom to the wise and knowledge to those who have understanding." That might be read as a simple affirmation of the divine source of human wisdom and knowledge. On the other hand, it might be an assertion that God gives divine wisdom and knowledge (only) to those who are capable of dealing with it. On this latter understanding, in other words, it is Daniel's exceptional wisdom and, in the words of chapter 1, "understanding in all visions and dreams," that makes him a fit recipient for this additional knowledge from God.

Of course Daniel, with typical diplomacy (cf. vs. 14), says nothing to the king of needing to save his own skin and takes care to elevate the role of the king as the recipient of knowledge rather than Daniel. What Daniel's speech *says* and what it *does*, however, are two different things. Daniel's speech *says* that Nebuchadnezzar is wrong to rely on his (human) sages when the only one who can help him is a god. But what Daniel's speech *does* is to point out to Nebuchadnezzar that he has merely relied on the wrong sages. If he had, from the beginning, depended upon someone like Daniel, his problem would have been solved long ago without the distasteful threats.

The dream that Daniel recounts to Nebuchadnezzar is a narrative within a narrative. Daniel takes us back to the moment of Nebuchadnezzar's dreaming by telling the dream from the king's point of view. Daniel begins the account by addressing the king in the second person, "You, O King, were looking . . . ," but immediately shifts to seeing the dream through the king's eyes: ". . . and, lo!—a great image!" Though Daniel verbalizes the dream, we see the dream as Nebuchadnezzar had seen it on that restless night.[3]

Interpreting the Dream: Verses 31-45

The dream (vss. 31-35) opens with a great and frightening image standing before Nebuchadnezzar. The image is a human form with a head of gold, chest and arms of silver, belly and thighs of bronze, legs of iron, and feet partly of iron and partly of clay. The image remains visible until a stone is cut, but not with human hands, and it strikes the image upon its feet and breaks them in pieces. Then, the entire image breaks into pieces and the wind carries the refuse away until nothing of the image remains. At this point, the stone becomes a great mountain and fills the whole earth.

Daniel shifts out of the dream and back into the context of its telling by saying, "This is the dream and we will tell its interpretation before the king" (vs. 36). The interpretation (vss. 37-45) draws connections both between the dream and the surrounding narrative and between the dream and events that will supposedly occur beyond the time narrated in the story. In other words, the dream both reflects the story world and temporally transcends it: The dream has both synchronic and diachronic significance.

Daniel's first explanatory comment associates the dream image with Nebuchadnezzar's present reign:

> "You, O king, king of kings, to whom the God of heaven has given the kingdom, the power, the might, and the honor, and into whose hand he has given all that dwell—human beings, beasts of the field, birds of the heaven—and he has caused you to rule over all of them: You are the head of gold." (2:37-38)

Daniel's words correlate the Nebuchadnezzar's vast dominion with the golden head of the dream image. Daniel's explanation, like the image itself, employs height and hierarchy to communicate the extent of power. As the head sits at the top of the body, so Nebuchadnezzar rules over the natural world ("all that dwell—human beings, beasts of the field, birds of the heaven . . .") and the political world ("king of kings" having "kingdom, power, might, and honor"). Daniel's words, however, also point out a part of the hierarchy that Nebuchadnezzar has not seen, either in his dream or in his life. The "God of heaven" stands over the "head of gold." The God of heaven "gives" control and "causes rule."

The rest of Daniel's interpretation is exclusively in terms of time. He connects the various elements of the dream to events that will occur after the present story has ended, indeed, after Nebuchadnezzar's reign has ended (when "the time has changed"!). The remaining anatomical parts of the image, presented from the shoulders to the feet and made from a series of different (mostly metallic) elements, represent a succession of kingdoms that will arise after Nebuchadnezzar's reign. Superiority is conveyed through hierarchy and the relative values of the metals. Each kingdom is inferior to the one preceding, although it is not made clear in what way this inferiority manifests itself except in the case of the last kingdom. The last kingdom, which begins with legs of iron and ends in feet of iron and pottery, starts with strength, but becomes too diverse and finally loses the strength that comes with unity. The stone is an indestructible kingdom established by the God of heaven. It puts an end to these other kingdoms and it stands forever.

After interpreting the dream, Daniel adds, "A great God has made known to the king what is to be after this . . ." (vs. 45), and thus condenses the dream to its diachronic dimensions. The dream is the future that the God of heaven wants Nebuchadnezzar to see. The future contains a confrontation between human power and divine power in which divine power will be victorious. The God of heaven wants Nebuchadnezzar to recognize the supremacy of divine power.

The problem with this exclusively temporal reading, however, is that the supremacy of divine power is an *eventual* supremacy, not a supremacy that is easily recognized in the present structure of things. By reading the dream primarily as a vision of the future, Daniel has minimized its judgmental nature. If the stone that crushes is, to Nebuchadnezzar, a disturbing image, then upon Daniel's temporal reading, he, like Hezekiah, can comfort himself with the thought, "Why not, if there will be peace and security in my days?" (2 Kgs 20:19). Small wonder, then, that his response to Daniel's interpretation is so benign. Daniel's somewhat one-sided view of the dream's content suggests to him that he need not be concerned with the destructive element of the dream: This will not happen in his lifetime. Thus, he easily turns his attention from the content of the dream to Daniel's remarkable ability to recount and interpret it.

Daniel is one who tells the truth but not the whole truth. Daniel's reading of the dream is an underreading. There are elements in the dream for which he has not given account to the king. The image, though built of multiple components, is still a singular entity, a unified structure that stands as one and falls as one. As a singular construct, its temporality is marked, not by succession, but by synchrony.[4]

Furthermore, Daniel never explains the significance of the image's human form or the contrast between the giant human figure and the stone which is cut, pointedly, without human hands. When Daniel speaks of the stone, he describes it as another kingdom raised up by the God of heaven, its distinction being that it will not be taken over by another people (vs. 44). The difference between the kingdom represented by the stone and those represented by the various metals is not noted as a difference in kind. It is not, according to Daniel's interpretation, a divine kingdom as opposed to a human one, for instance—the God of heaven has also raised up the "head of gold" and we know that, in Daniel's view, the God of heaven raises up all kings (vs. 21). Rather, the difference is its longevity, which is implicitly the result of its immense power.

The contrast between the gigantic human form and the stone uncontaminated by human chisel may be seen as more striking in the dream itself than it is in Daniel's interpretation. In a more synchronic reading of the dream, the accent falls more readily on the inherent tension created by the distinction. The image is shaped like a human body. It is composed of elements usually worked by human hands and valued by human society—gold and silver that adorn and give economic power, bronze and iron that make tools and weapons, and even pottery so necessary for literary and domestic purposes. The image is an idol, not of a divine being (cf. Siegmann), but of humanity. The top-heavy image is a symbol of a humanity that has over-reached itself. Juxtaposed to the human image is a power completely devoid of human characteristics, a force that is completely "other." The stone is a natural element that does rather unnatural things. It divorces itself from its surroundings, it propels itself against the image, it grows as if an organic entity, into a mountain that fills the entire earth. The mountain, in contrast to the image, is raw and undomesticated. It represents something that cannot be tamed by human power.[5]

The dream, of course, has a personal dimension as well. Daniel touches upon this when he identifies Nebuchadnezzar as the head of gold. The unstable image, with its glory and its commonality, its strength and its weakness, also represents the rule of Nebuchadnezzar. It is an awe-inspiring rule with a fragile foundation. If, as Daniel himself suggests, we see the dream as a product of Nebuchadnezzar's head ("the thoughts of [his] heart" [vs. 30]) as well as a communication from God, a reading that understands the king's character to be plagued by political uncertainty gains credibility.[6] The dream reflects worry. Is his control truly secure? Are those beneath him really dependable? Might they not make unexpected alliances (vs. 43)? Might they not rise up and crush authority (vs. 40)?[7]

The revealed content of the dream invites the reader to recall the initial scene involving the king and his sages. Now that we know the dream, we better understand his conversation. Why test his sages? Why the paranoid accusation "Undoubtedly you are buying *time* . . . . You have agreed with one another to speak a false and corrupt word before me *until the time has changed*" (vs. 8)? Perhaps political suspicion. The dream suggests a fear that time will not be kind to his reign. Why threaten dismemberment and destroyed house? Perhaps that is what he fears for himself and his kingdom—the image in his dream is certainly "dismembered." Why the wording, "there is but one sentence for all of you"? Perhaps he echoes what he has seen in his dream, that there is but one sentence for all the image's parts. Could the ominous vision of what might be his own end now make him wield his power with an even heavier hand? If so, he is fulfilling the dream's symbolism, deifying his own power, claiming autonomy over life and death.

If, as a product of Nebuchadnezzar's head, the dream represents both his hope and his fear—his hope of a magnificent, golden rule, but his fear of failure—and if, as a message from the God of heaven, the dream passes judgment upon his hubris, then Daniel's explanation of the dream has fallen short of the dream itself. By interpreting the dream as a vision of the future, by conveying the judgment as a judgment against the whole of political history, Daniel minimizes Nebuchadnezzar's culpability.

Daniel's version of the dream is the version of diplomacy. Perhaps he is keeping in mind the king's volatile nature as he consistently elevates the king's importance. The king is the head of gold. He is the recipient of a special gift, the divine gift of the kingdom. He is the one chosen by the God of heaven. Even the dream marks his favored status: The God of heaven wants to impart to him this knowledge concerning the future. Daniel's very presence and ability to interpret are signs of God's interest in the king.

In this public encounter Daniel expresses complete allegiance to the king. Yet a reader may remember the prayer that Daniel sings in the privacy of his home. Daniel's prayer responds not simply to his belief that God has made the dream known to him; his prayer responds to the content of the king's dream. He gleefully thanks God for "changing the times and the seasons" and not only for "setting up kings" but for "allowing kings to pass away." Perhaps Daniel is looking forward, as Nebuchadnezzar earlier accuses the sages of doing, to a day when the "situation is changed." Daniel's private political hopes are more complex than those he is willing to express in public.

Nebuchadnezzar's Response: Verses 46-49

Since, throughout Daniel's speech, the reader has not been allowed to see the king's face, the moment of Nebuchadnezzar's reaction is rather climactic. If he were to suspect the synchronic as well as the diachronic significance of the dream, his response could easily be anger. It appears, however, that he has been mesmerized by Daniel's ability to recount the dream and convinced by Daniel's diplomatically temporal rendering of its meaning. His response is a mixture of relief and wonder. Perhaps Daniel's interpretation has been more favorable than he thought he could expect. Certainly, Daniel's ability to do what only a god can do fills him with awe, not to mention confusion. If only a god can recount the dream of another, then Daniel must, somehow, be divine. Thus, he falls upon his face before Daniel and worships him (*sgd;* cf. the use of this verb in Isa 44:15, 17, 19; 46:6; and throughout Daniel 3); and he commands that an offering (*minḥah*) and incense offering (*niḥoḥin*) be poured out (*nsk*) as a libation to him.[8]

At this point we might expect Daniel to clarify the situation, to explain to the king that he, Daniel, is not divine but simply a human agent. He does no such thing, however. His success in telling the dream has completely drowned out his disclaimer that it was not he but God who was responsible for the revelation of the mystery to him. Moreover, his acceptance of religious homage undercuts the dream's messages about human limitation, the need to recognize that human limitation, and the distinction between human and divine power.

Nebuchadnezzar's ambiguous confession, "Truly your god is god of gods and lord of kings and a revealer of mysteries that you are able to reveal this mystery" (vs. 47), marks further his theological confusion. In the first place, "god" is subordinated to Daniel: The deity in question is not the "God of heaven" but "your god." Secondly, Nebuchadnezzar's grammar leaves us wondering about his understanding. Is it *because* Daniel's god is god of gods that Daniel is able to reveal the mystery? Or is his god now god of gods *because* Daniel is able to reveal the mystery? Can divinity and humanity be distinguished? Judging from Nebuchadnezzar's reaction, obviously not.

The story's denouement is brief. Nebuchadnezzar puts Daniel in charge of the entire province of Babylon and appoints him to be chief prefect over all the sages of Babylon (vs. 48). Daniel, in turn, requests that the service of the province be passed to his friends, Shadrach, Meshach, and Abednego. He keeps the role of leadership over the sages, however, and remains at the royal court (vs. 49).

It is at this point that the reader is likely to become disoriented. We seem to have here a version of how Daniel and his friends become successful in Nebuchadnezzar's administration that differs from chapter 1. If chapter 2 is to be read as a flashback, the narrator has been rather careless in the reestablishment of chronology. We might have expected Daniel and his friends to return and finish their training; instead, they are immediately incorporated into court life and promoted to high position. Thus, the two versions stand in tension with one another and raise the question of the narrator's reliability.[9] Does Daniel become successful because his special wisdom and ability are of constant, but general assistance to Nebuchadnezzar, as the narrator tells us in chapter 1? Or does Daniel become successful because, on this particular occasion, he so impresses the king with his ability and diplomacy that the king mistakes him for divine and his partial truth for the whole truth?

Chapter Three

DANIEL 3
THE KING'S PUBLIC IMAGE

Nebuchadnezzar's Image
Verses 1-7

Unlike the stories in chapters 1 and 2 which ease the reader into their worlds with orientation in time and place, chapter 3 begins abruptly.[1] "Nebuchadnezzar the king made an image of gold . . . ." As with Daniel's first mention in chapter 2, the narrator here assumes that we already know who Nebuchadnezzar is and, consequently, does not introduce him. The story is the continuation of a larger story. Furthermore, just as the narrator links our interest in chapters 1 and 2 with the subject of dreams, so here the narrator links chapter 3 to chapter 2 with the image of gold.

In describing this image the narrator leaves some gaps. We are told only of its size and location. We are not told what it symbolizes or why the king builds it. The association of this artifact with the image in Nebuchadnezzar's dream, however, invites the reader to fill these gaps with inferences from Daniel 2.[2] The identical word (*ṣelem*), comparable size, and matching component of gold prompt us to understand that Nebuchadnezzar is duplicating, though with some variation, the image he has seen in his dream. Taken by Daniel's interpretation that he himself is the head of gold, Nebuchadnezzar builds a corresponding image of gold. His created image remedies the weaknesses inherent in his dream-image: His is made of a unified substance; his has no feet of clay. If, according to Daniel's temporal reading of his dream, Nebuchadnezzar's rule is to be remembered as the golden age, then perhaps Nebuchadnezzar's structure should be interpreted as a visual symbol of the way in which he wants himself and his reign to be perceived, both now and in the years to come (cf. Anderson, 29-30; Baldwin, 99).

That the king is preoccupied with public perceptions is verified in his next action.

> And Nebuchadnezzar the king sent to assemble the satraps, the prefects and the governors, the counsellors, the treasurers, the judges, the officials and all the authorities of the province to come to the dedication of the image which Nebuchadnezzar the king had erected. (3:2)

No sooner is the long-winded list uttered than it is repeated in the narrator's report of the officials' arrival:

> Then the satraps, the prefects and the governors, the counsellors, the treasurers, the judges, the officials and all the authorities of the province assembled themselves for the dedication of the image which Nebuchadnezzar the king had erected. (3:3)

On the surface, this (almost) verbatim repetition of the list tells us precisely who is summoned and precisely who appears at the dedication of the image. It gives a guide to the nature of the gathering. All the people involved are identified by political status. This is not an occasion for the general populace; it is an administrative assembly. The list's extent suggests a rather sophisticated political network. The repetition of the list, however, also enacts the power structure of the story world. It shows the king's control of this network. Precisely what the king wills is precisely what takes place. The precise people whom he summons are the precise people who assemble. Thus, through repetition, the narrator pictures a setting in which conformity is normative, disobedience is unthinkable.

The repetition slows the pace of narration and the list's content broadens our range of vision. We began with a view limited to the king and his tremendous image; now our vision is broadened to include not only the king and his image, but also the assembled multitude.

While we look upon the crowd with our wide-angle vision, we hear the herald announce:

> "Oh, peoples, nations, and languages! When you hear the sound of the horn, the pipe, the lyre, the trigon, the harps, the bagpipes, and every kind of music, you will fall down and pay homage to the gold

image that Nebuchadnezzar the king has erected. Whoever does not fall down and pay homage will immediately be cast into the midst of a blazing fiery furnace." (3:4-6)

The dedication, it seems, involves more than gathering to admire the king's handiwork. The people are required to swear an allegiance to this image that is akin to worship.[3] If they refuse, they are sentenced to death by burning. By threatening death (cf. Dan 2:5, 9, 12), Nebuchadnezzar attempts to assert his control. But why is it so important that everyone present worship the image? Is it a god? We are not expressly told so. In fact the only clause qualifying it describes it as the image "that Nebuchadnezzar the king has erected." The frequent recurrence of this phrase (vss. 2, 3 [twice], 5, 7, 12, 14, 15, 18) suggests that, indeed, the image's significance lies in the fact that Nebuchadnezzar has made it. It is his accomplishment.[4]

The herald's address may also be of help in deciphering the import of the situation. When the herald addresses the congregation, we might have expected: "O satraps, prefects and governors, etc." Instead, he makes a substitution: "O peoples, nations, and languages!" When reporting the congregation's obedience to the order (vs. 7), the narrator also employs the herald's terminology: "all the peoples, nations, and languages fell down and paid homage . . . ." While the list of political offices identifies the people with the Babylonian administration, and thus signals affinity, the variation "peoples, nations and languages" acknowledges a broad national spectrum and thus signals difference. The people may be part of the Babylonian political structure, but they are also from a variety of national backgrounds. They represent nations who have been conquered and subjugated. To worship the image is to swear allegiance to Nebuchadnezzar. The dedication is a maneuver on Nebuchadnezzar's part to rally political solidarity.[5] Even the religious nuances of the dedication fit well into the promotion of political unity. One need only recall the reforms of Hezekiah and Josiah to understand that religious homogeneity and political autonomy go hand in hand.

The construction of the great image for the purpose of political control accords with our reading of chapter 2 in which Nebuchadnezzar is a king plagued by political insecurity. His dream, while reflecting his anxiety, has also given him an idea on how to relieve his anxiety. The image will be a standard of allegiance; the image will be the measure of his control. Thus, when he builds the image of gold, the reader knows that he has not understood the dream at all, except as it suits him. He seems to see the need to make himself the head of gold, to show himself superior to all other rulers; he does not see himself as part of the history of political hubris that stands condemned. His self-serving understanding legitimates the judgmental message of the dream. By erecting the image that represents his sovereignty, and by requiring that his officials worship the image, he has raised himself to the divine status for which the dream, on a broader reading, has condemned him.

The narrator's tone ridicules Nebuchadnezzar's misappropriation of the dream and this attempt to reassure himself of his powerful control. The tedious repetitions (of which we have not heard the last) undermine the solemnity of the occasion and leave the reader wondering about the hierarchy of significance in this story world of politics and power. Rather than explaining what the image represents, the narrator spends time repeatedly listing officials and musical instruments. The pomp of the event is given more emphasis than the meaning of the event. As noted above, the narrator constantly reminds us, as if we could forget at any moment, that the image is something "Nebuchadnezzar the king has erected." Thereby the king's attempt to be remembered as the head of gold is mocked.[6]

When reporting the crowd's response to the command, the narrator includes the seemingly redundant catalogue of musical instruments and echoes the herald's use of the nomenclature "peoples, nations, and languages." The narrator, however, adds the word *all*—"all the peoples, nations, and languages bowed down and worshipped the gold image . . . ." The addition of "all" produces several effects. "All" emphasizes the wholesale compliance of the assembly and thus accentuates the point made by the earlier repeated list of the officials: Precisely what the king commands is precisely what happens. The wholesale compliance of the assembly can put the king's political worry to rest.

Or can it? Does the word "all" represent the narrator's point of view? Might it not represent only Nebuchadnezzar's perspective? And might the narrator, by using the absurd repetition, be ridiculing the king's perspective that he has now attained the unanimous allegiance of his subjects?

The word "all" unsettles the reader and raises the question of point of view because our interest thus far has been focused on Daniel and his friends. On last report, Daniel and, subsequently, Shadrach, Meshach, and Abednego had been appointed as officials over the province of Babylon. The narrator tells us that all the officials of the province are present at this dedication (vs. 3). If Daniel and his friends would not even eat food from the king's table for fear of compromising authority, would they indeed now bow down and worship an image as a gesture of political allegiance?

Certain Chaldeans and Certain Jews: Verses 8-12

Suddenly, the scene shifts and the scope of our vision narrows. We are made to focus on "certain Chaldeans" (*gubrîn kasdâ'în*) who come forth and accuse "certain Jews" (*gubrîn yehûdâ'în*) of disobeying the royal order. Since the behavior of "certain Jews" is on our minds, we are not terribly surprised by this turn in the plot. As they speak, we realize that, if the Chaldean's testimony is reliable, our vantage point in the first scene (vss. 2-7) has been so distant that we have missed some of what must have taken place. Our view of the crowd has been so broad that we have not been able to see individuals. Furthermore, if the Chaldeans are telling the truth, our suspicion that the report of wholesale compliance (vs. 7) represents the king's point of view (and not the narrator's) gains in credence.

The scene in which Nebuchadnezzar learns of the disobedience of the three Jews could have been handled in several ways. The story could have read at this point, "And it was told to King Nebuchadnezzar that the Jews he had appointed over the affairs of the province of Babylon, Shadrach, Meshach, and Abednego, had refused to pay homage to the image which he had erected." Or the king, while officiating at the dedication, could have simply witnessed the disobedience himself.

Instead, our narrator, who never seems to miss the chance of a verbose repetition, introduces another party to give the report to the king. However, though they mimic the herald (vss. 4-6) and the narrator (vs. 7) before them, they offer their own version:

> "You, O King, have given a command that everyone who hears the sound of the horn, the pipe, the lyre, the trigon, the harp, the bagpipes, and every kind of music must fall down and pay homage to the gold image, and whoever does not fall down and pay homage will be

> cast into the midst of a blazing fiery furnace. There are certain Jews whom you appointed over the service of the province of Babylon—Shadrach, Meshach, and Abednego—these men, O King, show no deference to you. They do not serve your gods and they do not pay homage to the gold image that you have erected." (3:10-12)

The Chaldeans' account is what may be termed a *deliberate* variation of the original material. Regarding this type of variation, Meir Sternberg (422) writes:

> The deliberately variant retrospect often plays an . . . active part in biblical dialogue, one that subsumes "tactful" reference as a gambit, softening-up flattery, or snare for the addressee. The speaker's deviations then make sense in terms of his endeavor to move, persuade or impose his will on his interlocutor by contriving an *ad hominem* version of an antecedent speech or event.

In the case of the Chaldeans, they expand and, to a certain extent, reorganize the material in order to move the king to take action against the three Jews. As they reiterate the king's order, they carefully include the condition of disobedience (which the narrator, in reporting compliance in vs. 7, logically omitted). Since their purpose is to inform on Shadrach, Meshach, and Abednego, the pointed reminder of the fiery furnace is a subtle challenge to Nebuchadnezzar to act upon his word.

In their first mention of the gold image, the Chaldeans leave out the accompanying phrase, "that you have erected." This omission is striking because in every other occurrence of "the gold image," this phrase, or a variation of it, is present. The Chaldeans do not omit the phrase entirely, however, but they move it to the end of their speech, leaving the king to linger on the personal affront involved in the Jews' disobedience and reminding the king that it is this affront that provides grounds for execution according to the royal decree.

The main addition that the Chaldeans make in their speech is, of course, the information about Shadrach, Meshach, and Abednego.[7] The Chaldeans do not simply say, "These men did not pay homage to the gold image." They first mention the political position that these three hold: They are the king's personal appointees over the administration of the province of Babylon. As the Chaldeans continue, they craftily voice the affront as a personal one. Notice that they do not say, "These men show no deference to the royal decree" or "to Babylonian law." They do not refer to the divine as "Babylonian gods" or "our gods."

They pointedly make the king the target of the affront by employing the second person singular: "to *you*," "*your* gods," "the image *you* have erected." Their speech turns political betrayal into personal betrayal. In other words, the king himself appointed them to office and now they blatantly disregard his authority.

The Chaldeans attempt to discredit Shadrach, Meshach, and Abednego further by stressing their national and religious difference. They are Jews and "they do not serve your gods . . . ." (Thus, they echo with force the religious issue that was but a nuance in the exposition. They have made explicit Nebuchadnezzar's implicit presupposition regarding the dedication: Religious affinity is political affinity and, conversely, religious difference is political difference.) The Chaldeans' tacit equation is: Different is suspect.

The final evidence for the Jews' personal and political betrayal is their disobedience: ". . . and they do not pay homage to the gold image that you have erected." Thus, the Chaldeans plant the idea that the failure of the three to pay homage is the manifestation of their *complete* untrustworthiness—they show *no deference* to the king.[8] Consequently, if the king has had any inclination to make an exception for these three, this portrayal is designed to make him think twice.

In their rhetoric before the king, the Chaldeans implicitly contrast themselves to the three Jews. By informing the king of the Jews' disobedience, they imply their own obedience. By reporting that Shadrach, Meshach, and Abednego do not serve the king's gods or the image he has erected, they suggest that they themselves are of the same religious persuasion as the king. Through this rhetorical maneuver they align themselves with the king. They present themselves as dutiful subjects who have only the king's interests in mind.

The Chaldeans' presentation of themselves raise, in the reader's mind, the question of their motive(s). Why do they deem it necessary to inform on the Jews? Do they truly come forward out of religious piety and concern for the king, as the surface of the narrative suggests? Court "tattling" appears to be a popular motif in later Jewish literature. Often the informants are involved in framing the victim and misleading the king out of political jealousy or personal hatred (cf. Daniel 6; Esther 3). In Daniel 3 the Chaldeans appear to be merely acting upon what they have seen. Lest the audience be carried away by the Chaldeans' presentation of themselves as dutiful subjects, however, the narrator warns against such simplistic interpretation with the phrase "ate the pieces of," that is, "maliciously accused" the Jews. Thus, the narrator leaves no doubt of the Chaldeans' hostility toward the Jews.

The shape of the scene itself also provides a clue to the Chaldeans' motivation. Recall for a moment another court story involving someone who informs an unknowing king of rebellion at hand. In 1 Kings 1 when David's son Adonijah begins to prepare himself for kingship, Bathsheba (encouraged by Nathan the prophet) goes before the aged and ailing King David and speaks to him in terms not unlike those of the Chaldeans to Nebuchadnezzar. She begins by reminding (or so she claims) the king that he has sworn an oath and by repeating that oath:

> "My lord, you swore to your maidservant by Yahweh your God saying, 'Solomon your son shall reign after me, and he shall sit upon my throne.' " (1 Kgs 1:17)

The Chaldeans in Daniel 3 begin in much the same way with a reminder and a repetition:

> "You, O King, have given a command that everyone who hears the sound of the horn, the pipe, the lyre, the trigon, the harp, the bagpipes, and every kind of music must fall down and pay homage to the gold image and whoever does not fall down and pay homage will be cast into the midst of a blazing fiery furnace."

In 1 Kgs 1:18, Bathsheba continues with the actual information that she came to impart to the king:

> "And now, behold, Adonijah is king, although you, my lord the king, do not know it."

Bathsheba then elaborates:

> "He has sacrificed oxen, fatlings, and sheep in abundance, and has invited all the sons of the king, . . . but Solomon your servant he has not invited."

At the same structural point, the Chaldeans also share their critical information (Dan 3:12):

> "There are certain Jews whom you appointed over the administration of the province of Babylon—Shadrach, Meshach, and Abednego—These men, O King show no deference to you."

The Chaldeans also offer an elaboration of their accusation:

> "They do not serve your gods and they do not pay homage to the gold image that you have erected."

Bathsheba's words make it clear that the reason for such a speech is to move the king to action: "And now, my lord the king, the eyes of all Israel are upon you, to tell them who shall sit on the throne of my lord the king after him . . ." (1 Kgs 1:20). The Chaldeans, however, leave their speech open, leading the king to recognize for himself that "the eyes of all Babylon" are upon him to see if he will carry out his threat or not. The analogy between the two scenes is further reinforced by the same protocol formula. The Chaldeans preface their speech with adulation: "O King, live forever!" Bathsheba responds likewise to David's promise to make her son king: "May my lord King David live forever!"

In 1 Kings 1 Bathsheba clearly does not come forward with her information just because she feels obligated to be the eyes and ears of the king. She does not even do so out of hatred for Adonijah: Her feelings about him are never made explicit. Rather she has a personal and political motive. Adonijah occupies the position that she desires for her son. So she portrays Adonijah, whether truthfully or not we cannot be sure, as a usurper. And thus she discredits him. In contrast, the character of Solomon emerges from her speech as the patient son, loyal to the end, the true servant of the king and, consequently, the more attractive candidate for kingship.

Although the corresponding scene in Daniel 3 is not as explicit as that of 1 Kings 1, the Chaldeans present their case in much the same way with a similar goal in mind. The Chaldeans are not interested in simply turning in disobedient Jews; they are interested in turning in *particular* Jews—Jews whom the king himself has appointed to administer the province of Babylon. The implied argument is that, if Shadrach, Meshach, and Abednego show no deference to the king in this matter, they are probably delinquent in other matters as well; thus they are unsuitable for their present political position. The Chaldeans themselves, on the other hand, are loyal in the matter at hand, loyal enough to report dissent and would certainly make suitable administrators over the province of Babylon.

The King and the Jews: Verses 13-18

From what we know of Shadrach, Meshach, and Abednego from chapter 1, the reader suspects that the three may indeed be guilty of disobeying the king's order. Following Daniel's lead, the three refused the indenturing royal food; it seems most likely that they have also refused to worship the image. What they might do when publicly challenged on this issue is another matter, however. After all, Daniel is not around to take charge. Besides, discrete disobedience is remarkably easier than overt defiance.

What the king believes about Shadrach, Meshach, and Abednego is unclear, but he does not accept the Chaldeans' report unquestioningly. He calls the three before him and questions them concerning the truth of the accusation. But because he does not pause for an answer at this point, the reader is left in suspense as to their reaction. Instead, the king continues on, offering them the opportunity to prove the Chaldeans incorrect. He recreates the situation to see their response for himself.

Here, the fourth repetition of the edict occurs in yet another context of communication with yet another set of characters. Each repetition has brought us a step closer to the central confrontation of the story. With this fourth and final repetition there are no mediators—no herald speaking on the king's behalf, no narrator reporting obedience, no Chaldeans reporting disobedience. The king and the Jews are face to face.

Having just listened to the Chaldeans' rhetoric and facing the suspected dissidents, the king varies his version of the order accordingly:

> "Is it true, Shadrach, Meshach, and Abednego, that you do not serve my gods nor do you pay homage to the gold image that I have erected? Now, if you are ready, when you hear the sound of the horn, the pipe, the lyre, the trigon, the harp, the bagpipes and every kind of music, you will fall down and pay homage to the image that I have made. If you do not pay homage, you will promptly be cast into the midst of a blazing fiery furnace. And who is the god who will deliver you from my hands?" (3:14-15)

Nebuchadnezzar changes the order of the material and also makes an addition. Rather than giving the command straight away, he first echoes, in a question to the three, the last statements of the Chaldeans. Then, rather than waiting for an answer, he hurries on with the command. What it all boils down to, he seems to be hinting, is their performing the act of paying homage. He is less concerned with their belief than he is with their conduct. They may not believe in his gods; they may put no stock in the image that he has made; but they should at least bow down out of respect for and fear of the king. He deserves their homage because he has the power to put them to death. He challenges what he correctly perceives to be their loyalty to their own god: "Who is the god who will deliver you from my hands?" The object of such loyalty should be powerful. He himself is ultimately powerful because he can have them killed; their god cannot possibly compare. Thus, he attempts to persuade them by pointing out their misplaced loyalty and by playing upon their fear.

Shadrach, Meshach, and Abednego are no longer three faceless people in the obscurity of a multitude. They stand alone, front and center. Whatever they do now determines what becomes of them. Suspense builds as we wait through the king's listing of musical instruments, his threat for disobedience, his gibe at the folly of their position should they indeed prove to be recalcitrant: "And who is the god who will deliver you from my hands?"

Where the tension is highest, our vision is the narrowest. There is nothing in the scene to distract us (no account of the Chaldeans' smug reaction, for example, or no mention of other characters who are spectators of this incident). We are not even allowed to see all four characters at once, except in verse 13. We see and hear Nebuchadnezzar first with blinders toward Shadrach, Meshach, and Abednego. Then our sight and hearing are limited exclusively to the three whom we could not even spot in the first scene. Not until they finish are we allowed to learn Nebuchadnezzar's reaction to them.

The speech of Shadrach, Meshach, and Abednego in verses 17-18 (and it is their only one) marks the first and the major climactic point in the story. Their speech breaks the verbal rules, so to speak. Their speech is set apart from all the others heard thus far in that they refuse to answer with the extensive repetition that has become so common in the story. Not only do they fail to use full-scale repetition themselves, they speak without waiting for the musical signal and thus deprive the narrator of the final chance to relist the instruments.

The response of Shadrach, Meshach, and Abednego does echo

smaller segments of the earlier material. Their selectivity allows the three to answer concisely; they do not attempt to buy time. They offer no self defense. Instead, they direct their response to the king's closing question, using many of his same terms. The king himself intends a rhetorical question to which the implied answer is: "There is no god who can deliver from your hand." Shadrach, Meshach, and Abednego, however, refuse to interpret it as rhetorical. They address the question by affirming loyalty, not to Nebuchadnezzar, but to their god:

> "If our god, whom we serve, is able to deliver us from a blazing fiery furnace and from your hand, O King, then he will deliver. But if not, be it known to you, O King that we would not serve your gods nor would we pay homage to the gold image that you have erected." (3:17-18)

Their words overpower the words of the king. By refusing to acknowledge his rhetoric, they render his speech impotent. By assuming his prescribed punishment (they do not beg for mercy), they emasculate his threat.

Furthermore, their response separates all the issues that have been fused together by the king and the Chaldeans before him. The issues of deliverance and divine ability are distinguished from the decision between loyalty and idolatry. Whether or not their god is able to deliver, they will not succumb to idolatry or tyranny. Their action is independent of the action of their god. Their loyalty is not contingent upon his power.[9]

Thus Shadrach, Meshach, and Abednego repeat elements of the king's speech—"deliver," "fiery furnace," "your hand," "[we] do not serve your gods," "[we] do not pay homage to the gold image that you have erected"—in such a way as to reexpress the issues in their own terms. For Nebuchadnezzar there is no viable alternative to serving his gods and worshipping his image. For Shadrach, Meshach, and Abednego, there is no viable alternative to "our god whom we serve."

Consequently, the words of Shadrach, Meshach, and Abednego put the king in his place, his human place, and they are a judgment upon his hubris. Though the three Jews may be uncertain about their god's *ability* to deliver them, they are confident that their god is *willing* to deliver them.[10] Their confidence communicates something about the nature of their god. Whether or not their god is omnipotent, their god still has a sense of fidelity, justice, righteousness. These are qualities that, obviously, the king does not have. Their confidence in divine willingness is a confession of faith that, if their god is able to right this evil, unjust situation, then indeed their god will.

The scene in which Shadrach, Meshach and Abednego stand before the king parallels the preceding scene involving the Chaldeans before their sovereign (Kuhl, 18). In both cases the visual picture is the same: subjects standing before their king. Both parties are given similar designations. The informers are called "certain Chaldeans." In their speech they refer to Shadrach, Meshach, and Abednego as "certain Jews."

Comparison, however, invites contrast. The Chaldeans stand before the king portraying loyalty to his highness. Shadrach, Meshach, and Abednego stand before the king confessing loyalty to a higher authority. The Chaldeans adopt the king's religious practices in order to advance themselves personally and politically. Shadrach, Meshach, and Abednego refuse to adopt the king's religious practices even though it means sacrificing not just political station, but life itself. The Chaldeans appear to have nothing to lose (after all, they have only reported the truth) and everything to gain. The Jews appear to have everything to lose and nothing to gain.

The religious language exchanged between the king and three Jews ("you do not serve my gods" / "our god whom we serve") also provides a common ground for comparing the three subjects to their sovereign. In this case, the piety of the politically powerful stands in ironic contrast to the piety of the politically unprotected. For one, the object of devotion is subordinated—"the image that I have made." For the other, the object of devotion is absolute—"the god whom we serve." For one, religion involves personal elevation and political control. For the other, religion demands personal sacrifice and the forfeit of control. Both take a rigid stance. It takes less courage, however, to exercise power than to resist it.

Into the Fiery Furnace: Verses 19-23

As we have listened to the defiant speech of Shadrach, Meshach and Abednego, the narrator has given us no glimpse of Nebuchadnezzar. We are made to wait for his reaction. In verse 19 the narrator turns our attention to the king and observes that, at this point, the "image," that is, the expression, of Nebuchadnezzar's face changes toward the three men. By employing the same word, *ṣelem*, that has been used to refer to the image of gold, the narrator playfully connects the image of gold with the image of Nebuchadnezzar's face. The word play satirizes Nebuchadnezzar's audacity through allusion: In Genesis 1 Elohim creates humanity in the divine image (*ṣelem*); in Daniel 3 Nebuchadnezzar creates, in his own (very human) image, an object to be worshipped (and note in verse 28 that Nebuchadnezzar substitutes the word "god" for "image").

The changing of Nebuchadnezzar's "image," or expression, marks a turning point in the story. As the plot moves toward the seemingly certain execution, the narrator moves us away from the action. As the preparations are made for the men to be burned, we watch from a more distant position. Our perspective is broader, encompassing more space and more characters.

On a first reading, we anticipate an execution because the story has promised it. The king has threatened it, the Chaldeans have forced it, the Jews have accepted it.[11] Readers may be familiar with the theme, "The king's fury is a messenger of death" (Prov 16:14), not only from their experience of the world, but also from stories like 2 Samuel 12 and Daniel 2 that mimic human experience of power structures. Readers may also be aware that, in the larger story of Israel, people have been known to die by fire for any number of reasons (for example, Achan's household in Joshua 7; Jephthah's daughter in Judges 11; Zedekiah and Ahab in Jer 29:22).

Although prepared for an execution, readers may also recognize certain literary allusions in the story that allow for other possibilities. The king manipulatively asks in verse 15:

> "Who is the god who will deliver you from my hands?"

The question echoes Deuteronomy 32:39 in which Yahweh himself says:

> "There is no one who can deliver from my hand."

The question also brings to mind the story of Sennacherib's attempt to take Jerusalem in 2 Kgs 18:13–19:37 (Porteous, 59). Through the voice of his messenger, Sennacherib sends a similar taunt to the people of the city:

> "Has any of the gods of the nations ever delivered his land out of the hand of the king of Assyria? . . . Who among all the gods of the lands have delivered their land from my hand, that YHWH should deliver Jerusalem from my hand?" (2 Kgs 18:33, 35)

Both allusions prompt a reader to see the king's audacity and to realize that, though the king does not view himself so, the narrator is portraying him to be blasphemous. The 2 Kings passage, because it too is narrative, is particularly suggestive concerning the plot of Daniel 3. Sennacherib threatens to take Jerusalem, but a miracle occurs that keeps him from doing so. The allusion suggests an analogy, and thereby foreshadows what is to come in Daniel 3. A miraculous deliverance is a possible plot alternative. Based on the analogy, we might expect one that prevents the threatened punishment from taking place.

This expectation is supported by another possible allusion. In verses 19-21 the three men are bound in preparation for the burning. The binding and the fire are reminiscent of another binding for another fire, the binding of Isaac for a holocaust on Mount Moriah in Genesis 22 (Lacoque, 66). In that story, too, divine intervention prevents the destruction.

The Isaac story also invites us to see the sacrificial nature of the execution. The three Jews are bound to be burned as sacrifices, a turn of events foreshadowed in Daniel 1 by the king's command to select for royal service young Judean captives who were "without blemish."[12]

Standing in tension with the narrative elements that point to certain death, the allusions to miraculous deliverance may alert an imaginative reader to the possibilities and therefore the hope, if not expectation, of something happening to prevent the three from being thrown into the furnace. We look for something to happen to the king to cause him to change his mind, a divine voice, perhaps, or we hope for an angel to appear and extinguish the flames (Kuhl, 39).

As first-time readers we are pulled between that for which we are prepared, but which we fear, and that for which we hope. The narrator holds us in suspense, teetering between the two possibilities, unsure of what is to come. (On subsequent readings we are likely to savor the suspense less, the texture of the narrative more.) The preparations for the execution proceed with a meticulous cadence similar to that in the Genesis 22 story. The furnace is heated beyond customary proportion.

Strong men are selected from the army to conduct the execution. The three men are bound. Their state of dress is described to the last detail. And then, in the moment most likely for divine intervention to take place, the three are cast into the furnace. Suddenly the matter is closed, the men are gone, and with a stroke of finality, the narrator informs us that the men who threw them in are killed by the intensity of the flame. If those outside the furnace are slain, those cast in stand no chance.

It appears that the "certain strong men" (*gubrîn gibbârê-ḥayil;* vs. 20) and the "certain Jews" (*gubrîn yehûdâ'în;* vs. 12) are linked by more than the narrator's designation. They (appear at this point to) suffer the same fate and so enact the hazards of loyalty.

The deaths of the executioners is an ironic twist on the motif of retribution. The evil accuser who suffers the punishment intended for the hero may be typical of folktales—compare Haman in Esther 7, or Daniel's accusers in Daniel 6—but the variation here deserves closer attention. Why does the narrator have relatively innocent figures suffer the punishment rather than the more logical choices, the "certain" Chaldeans or even the king?

One answer is that simple retribution is not the issue here. These "certain strong men," like all the assembled officials in verse 7, are unquestioningly obedient to the king. Their obedience is contrasted to Shadrach, Meshach, and Abednego's calculated disobedience to the king and, at the same time, compared with the three's obedience to their god. The executioners die meaningless deaths in obedience to an unconcerned sovereign with limited power. Nebuchadnezzar cannot control the killing. Even if he were to want to, Nebuchadnezzar is not able to deliver his loyal subjects from his own "hand," that is, the blazing fiery furnace.

Nebuchadnezzar and the Furnace: Verses 24-27

After this second climactic moment, there is a pause in which we are left to ponder the monstrosity that we have just witnessed.[13] The story could easily end at this point; the plot is complete for a martyr story. The nature of the climactic event, however, is stirring rather than settling. Although we had been prepared for this possibility, we hunger for justice (Kuhl, 38-39).

When the narrative resumes, our thoughts are on the three men in the fire, but the narrator forces our attention to Nebuchadnezzar. Although something is happening in the furnace, we are only allowed to watch Nebuchadnezzar's response to it.[14] We see his alarm, but not its source. We wait with wonder as he questions his counsellors, "Did we not cast three bound men into the midst of the fire?" and they give answer, "It is true, O King." In verse 25 Nebuchadnezzar announces what he sees, and the reader, too, is taken by surprise:

> "Lo, I see four men, unbound, walking around in the midst of the fire and no harm has come to them! And the appearance of the fourth is like that of a son of the gods." (3:25)

What we might have thought had been settled has not been settled at all. Execution is not the last word.

If we had hoped for deliverance *from* the fire, we had probably not expected deliverance *within* the fire. But, if so, perhaps we should have considered the option. Since fire often accompanies theophany in the Hebrew Bible (for example, Exod 3; 13:21-22, Num 16:35), we should have recognized earlier the irony involved in the choice of fire as a means of execution (Plöger, 63-64). We now can see that the often repeated phrase, "blazing fiery furnace," has been foreshadowing this outcome all along. Not only does a divine representative appear in the flames, but, like the burning bush, the men are not consumed.

This turn in the plot requires that the reader backtrack to the moment in which the three are cast into the furnace and in which the executioners are killed. The death of the executioners must now be reinterpreted. On the first reading, the deaths of the executioners appeared to dramatize the certain deaths of Shadrach, Meshach, and Abednego. But on second reading, the executioners' deaths render the subsequent miracle more impressive.

The images of the heroes surviving the fiery furnace and of one "like a son of the gods" joining them in the flames are so vivid that they are, for the most part, the images that make the story memorable. These intense images, however, do not function simply to impress the reader. Their central purpose is to make an impact on the story world and on Nebuchadnezzar in particular. These images are not allowed to overpower the reader because our point of view is immediately directed elsewhere.

In verse 26 Nebuchadnezzar summons the three men from the

furnace, calling them "servants of the highest god." They step forth from the fire, but rather than our attention being focused on them, our attention is directed to the perceptions of those gathered around. The assembled officials—"the satraps, the prefects and the governors and the king's counsellors"—witness that the men are completely untouched by the flames. Although not every group of officials is mentioned by name,[15] enough of the list is here to indicate that the same people who were called to worship the image are the very ones who witness the miraculous survival of the three Jews. Hence an irony—the assembly is called for one purpose, but an entirely different purpose is served. Nebuchadnezzar's intention for the dedication, like his intention to kill the three Jews, is thwarted. The gold image is forgotten.

Shadrach, Meshach, and Abednego say nothing else throughout the remainder of the story. We know nothing of their perceptions. They give us no account of their experience in the fire; they tell us nothing about the one "like a son of the gods." Their character is one that does not change through the course of the story. Even though the narrator has set up an ordeal structured like a rite of passage (see Chapter 1, above), a mythical hero's journey from old life to (symbolic) death to new life (Joseph Campbell has discussed this myth at length), the ordeal so designed to bring about change brings about none for those who participate in it. Their faith is no stronger. They acquire no new powers. Their unchanged appearance so deliberately stressed by the narrator is symbolic of their unchanged character.

Besides being static, the character of Shadrach, Meshach, and Abednego is, like all the other characters in the story with the exception of Nebuchadnezzar, collective. The "satraps, the prefects and the governors, the counsellors, the treasurers, the judges, the officials and all the authorities of the province," the "certain Chaldeans," the "certain strong men" from the royal army, and the king's counsellors all are completely uniform. They speak and act as one. No individual personalities emerge. Shadrach, Meshach, and Abednego, though they appear as heroic figures, are never portrayed as individuals.

Consequently, we may decide that the story is not their story. It is not a story of their heroism. The story is about the effect of their heroism on the world around them, and in particular, on the king who has tried to transform them and, failing that, has tried to kill them.[16]

The consistent collective and static characterization of Shadrach, Meshach, and Abednego, as well as of the others, highlights the single individual in the story, King Nebuchadnezzar. The narrator has focused our attention on Nebuchadnezzar more than on any other character and, for the remainder of the story he again fills our range of vision. As the only one to have seen inside the furnace (not even the narrator admits to having witnessed what has transpired there), Nebuchadnezzar is now the one who offers testimony. Ironically, it is he, rather than Shadrach, Meshach, and Abednego, who is changed by the ordeal by fire. He acquires a new knowledge and it is this acquisition of knowledge around which the story turns.[17]

As Nebuchadnezzar shares his new knowledge of God, we realize how dependent we are on the characters for *our* knowledge of this god. The deity who answers Nebuchadnezzar's challenge is not presented as a character in the story at all. We know the power of this god because we see Shadrach, Meshach, and Abednego unharmed by the fire. We know the presence of this god, because Nebuchadnezzar has reported seeing a divine representative. Just as in chapter 2, God's power has an effect on the story world, but God's character cannot be seen. Our vision of God in the story, like our vision of God in real life, is severely limited.

Nebuchadnezzar's Decree:
Verses 28-30

Nebuchadnezzar responds to what he has witnessed with "Blessed be the god of Shadrach, Meshach, and Abednego who . . . delivered his servants who . . . gave their bodies because they would not serve nor would they pay homage to any god except their god" (vs. 28). One might expect a version closer to the repetition we have heard before, something along the lines of "they would not serve my gods nor would they pay homage to the gold image I have erected." "My gods" and "the gold image that I have erected/made" have been preempted by "any god except their god." The king is fairly reticent about his own involvement in the preceding ordeal. By making the issue strictly a religious one, by omitting all political elements, by exempting himself from culpability, he saves face (or perhaps one should say "image").

The limits of Nebuchadnezzar's new knowledge become apparent as he continues his speech. As he does in chapter 2, the king defines and identifies the divine in terms of the human. Though he recognizes the power of the Judean god, he does not even inquire about the name or nature of the god. Instead, he refers to the deity as "the god of Shadrach, Meshach, and Abednego." While he expresses amazement concerning this god's might, he never admits that his own power should be subject to this divine power. In fact, he immediately attempts to exert control over this deity by issuing a royal decree:

> "I make a decree that any people, nation or language that says anything against the god of Shadrach, Meshach, and Abednego will be dismembered and his house will be laid in ruins because there is no other god who is able to deliver like this." (3:29)

The structural balance of the story lends an ironic force to the climactic confession of Nebuchadnezzar. This decree concerning the god of Shadrach, Meshach, and Abednego mirrors the earlier decree concerning the gold image. Both order some type of religious subservience. Both threaten death for disobedience. Nebuchadnezzar is again in the business of controlling the religious attitudes of others by wielding his political power.

While his first decree is commission, the king's second decree is prohibition. The people are not required to worship the god of Shadrach, Meshach, and Abednego; they are merely prohibited from saying anything against this god. Although he has witnessed a miracle, it seems that the king's allegiance to this god, like his knowledge of this god, has its limitations. Nevertheless, he makes this god politically useful. Like the gold image, this god becomes a measurement of political fidelity: Whoever speaks against this god shall be "punished as culprits against the realm" (Montgomery, 216).

The god of Shadrach, Meshach, and Abednego is now to be recognized because of the *deliverance* that has just taken place (vss. 28-29). The theme of deliverance harkens back to the king's question of deliverance in verse 15 and produces a fitting irony: The same character who mockingly asks "Who is the god who will deliver you from my hands?" is the one who answers his own question, "There is no other god who is able to deliver like this."

In verse 15 the king uses the verb *szb* ("deliver") which is repeated twice by Shadrach, Meshach, and Abednego (vs. 17). The verb occurs again in verse 28 when Nebuchadnezzar blesses the god of Shadrach, Meshach, and Abednego for delivering his servants. In his final statement in the story, Nebuchadnezzar confesses, ". . . there is no other god who is able to deliver like this." Here, however, instead of *szb* he uses the verb *nṣl*. This is not a deliberate substitution on the part of Nebuchadnezzar; the substitution is part of the narrator's rhetoric. The verb *nṣl* is the same verb used in 2 Kings 18 and 19, the same verb used in Deut 32:39: "See now that I, even I, am he, and there is no god beside me; I kill and I make alive; I wound and I heal; and there is none that can deliver out of my hand." Consequently, while Nebuchadnezzar comes to the realization that the god of Shadrach, Meshach, and Abednego is the "highest god," the narrator, behind the backs of the characters, is communicating to the reader the message that this god who delivers is indeed the only god.

The royal decree shows also that Nebuchadnezzar still considers himself to be in control of life and death. In godlike fashion, he still decides the destinies of his subjects. The coda of the story also plays upon this point. Verse 30 tells us that "the king made Shadrach, Meshach, and Abednego prosperous." The sound of the verb *haṣlaḥ*, "he made prosper," echoes the infinitive in the preceding verse, *lehaṣṣalah*, "to deliver." The play of sound between the two words connects the two ideas. The king now acts as the god acts. Those whom this god delivers, the king makes prosper.

For Shadrach, Meshach, and Abednego, the word play suggests another ironic turn. The three men are indebted to their god for deliverance. Are they now indebted to their king for prosperity? Has the king not obligated them after all?

The Story as Metaphor

Of this story, James Wharton (171-72) writes:

> [T]he story of the three men in the fire strikes us as a piece of surrealistic art. There is a kind of photographic realism about the way we are asked to imagine all the details of this story. Yet the net effect of the story is to call in question all our common sense perspectives about what is actually going on in the world. No tyrant is ever so explicitly anti-godly. No choice we make is ever quite so clear. No saint is ever so unambiguously saintly. No ending is ever quite as spectacularly happy as this one.

The reality of the story world in Daniel 3 stands in tension with what we perceive to be reality in the world around us. While we may "willingly suspend disbelief" in order to enter into the story world, we are not required to sustain disbelief when assessing what that world means for our world. For most readers, Daniel 3 does not imbue them with the confidence that, if they themselves were to walk into a fire for similar reasons, they would be miraculously protected from harm. Nor does Daniel 3 make most readers oblivious to the fact that, in the real world, people burn everyday in the resistance against tyranny. Most readers know that this is not the only story that can be told of religious persecution (cf. 2 Maccabees 7).

Might it not be that this story that is too good to be true, this story that speaks of unequaled tyranny, unsullied faith, unflinching heroism, and unquestionable divine presence is but a small paradigm of a larger story of ambiguous politics, compromised faith, confused response, and an elusive god? This story is a metaphor for exilic experience. André Lacocque (66) writes: ". . . the three companions are Israel in Exile saved through divine intervention." If this is a story of Israel in exile, then it must be recognized that this is an exceptionally clean story of clear choices made by model characters. As Wharton points out, our reality is not like that and, I suspect, neither was (is) the reality of exile. The story, however, selects and organizes, only telling part, never telling all, in an attempt to make sense of uncertainty, to see with clarity what is blurred in real life. In short, the story as metaphor offers an answer, offers a meaning, offers a lens with and through which we can read a difficult text—the text of exilic experience.

The key image of this metaphorical reading is that of the fiery furnace. Both "fire" and "furnace" are metaphors known from Israel's larger story, metaphors of captivity. In Deut 4:20, the exodus from Egypt is described in terms of Yahweh's bringing Israel out of an "iron furnace."[18] In a speech of comfort to those in exile, Deutero-Isaiah uses the metaphor of fire to describe the exilic experience: "When you pass through the waters I will be with you; and through the rivers, they shall not overwhelm you; when you walk through fire you shall not be burned, and the flame shall not consume you" (Isa 43:2). By analogy, the fiery furnace in Daniel 3 is symbolic of exilic experience and, as Lacocque has observed, the three friends are Israel faced with decision: They can conform and survive or retain their identity only to be persecuted and to die. As a metaphor, the story communicates that, despite all attempts to make them conform, the Jews endure exile unchanged, identity secure, integrity intact, loyal to their god.[19]

If Shadrach, Meshach, and Abednego had succumbed to Babylonian uniformity along with all the other "peoples, nations, and languages," they would have lost their identities as Jews and there would have been no story to tell (an issue also prominent in chapter 1). Likewise, if the Jews of the Babylonian exile (or any kind of exile for that matter) had conformed completely to the culture in which they found themselves, there would be no Jewish nation; there would be no story to tell. Consequently, chapter 3 is, on one level, a celebration of a nation's endurance.

On another level, the story is also an attempt to make sense of exilic experience, to reassess what it means to be Israel and to be in relationship with God. It portrays the exile as a test of both the people and God. For both Israel and God, exile tests fidelity. Can the people be faithful even when they cannot be assured of God's fidelity? Has God not abandoned them, "given them into the hand" of Nebuchadnezzar of Babylon? Will God, in the end, keep faith with Israel? From the people's perspective, exile is also a test of God's sovereignty. If Israel claims their God to be sovereign, will their God indeed prove to be so? Will God be able to deliver? And will God be able to deliver in such a way that Israel's fidelity will be justified in the eyes of other "peoples, nations, and languages"?

It is this third party that complicates the relationship between God and Israel. According to the metaphor of the story, exile is an opportunity for other "peoples, nations, and languages" to acquire a knowledge of God. The captivity and testing of Israel is not for Israel alone. Like the narrator of Daniel 3, God is concerned, perhaps primarily, with the perspectives of those outside Israel, particularly those outside Israel with political power. Israel's God has become ambitious. It is no longer enough to be recognized by Israel alone. In order to be sovereign of the world, God must catch bigger fish than Israel. Israel becomes the sacrifice, the burnt offering without blemish, that is to secure the victory, the recognition of God's sovereignty by "all peoples, nations and languages" (cf. the suffering servant passages in Isaiah 40-55).

Finally, the metaphor of chapter 3 suggests that, in exile, Israel discovers yet another side of their God. Their God's fidelity does not lie in preventing exile, just as in the story, God does not extinguish the fire or allow them to escape. Instead, their God joins them in the flames. As Lacocque (66) comments, "In Babylon as in Egypt, 'he is with them *in* distress' (Ps. 91:15) . . . ." God is "with them in distress" not simply for their own sake, but for the sake of those who cause and witness their distress and, ultimately, for the sake of God's name. God is with Israel in distress, "because he [Israel] knows my name" (Psalm 91:14). Israel and God's name are inextricably bound together. (After all, how can the god of Shadrach, Meshach, and Abednego be recognized if there is no Shadrach, Meshach and Abednego? How can the god of Israel be known if there is no Israel?) Israel's endurance depends upon divine presence, but might it not also be the case that divine presence is dependent upon Israel's endurance?

Chapter Four

DANIEL 4
THE KING'S PRAISES

"... the word of the king rules and who can say to him, 'What are you doing?' " (Eccl 8:4)

Nebuchadnezzar's Doxology: Verses 1-3 [3:31-33]

Our story this time orients us by first disorienting us. Cast as an official proclamation, the piece has an air of reality, an atmosphere of authority. The salutation indicates direct discourse:

> Nebuchadnezzar the king to all peoples, nations, and languages who dwell in all the earth: "May your peace be multiplied!" (4:1 [3:31])

In this first sentence the speaker identifies himself as Nebuchadnezzar the king. Because he does not limit himself to "king of Babylon," he implies that his kingship extends over all to whom he speaks—"all peoples, nations, and languages who dwell in all the earth." A ruler of the world commands attention. His communication is authoritative. The word of the king rules.

The address to all the people of the world is not without its ironies. Those specified are, of course, the audience within the story world, namely, the people under the rule of the character Nebuchadnezzar. That is to say, in the story world the king addresses his subjects, charging them to hear what he has to proclaim.

"All peoples, nations, and languages" can, however, have another referent. The phrase is broad enough to include the implied readers, the audience outside the story world to whom the story itself is directed as a communication. Although never vassals of Nebuchadnezzar, readers might also hear a direct address, a communication from a speaker who seems to "break the frame."[1] Hence, we may be called upon to adopt a more subjective relationship to the text than was necessary when reading chapters 1-3. The voice of the speaker is not that of our sovereign, but a voice from the grave, the voice of a king who once ruled but who rules no longer. Consequently, we may hear two communications, one that is internal to the story world, another that crosses the boundaries of the story world. The first is what the ruler of the world commands his subjects to hear; the second is the speech of a king long deceased to readers familiar with his fate.[2]

When, in verse 1 [3:31], Nebuchadnezzar extols before all the world the signs and wonders of the Most High God, we may think first that this praise results from the signs and wonders witnessed by the king in chapter 3. His address, "all peoples, nations, and languages," echoes his invocations regarding the gold image (3:4) and the god of Shadrach, Meshach, and Abednego (3:29). It would make sense that, after reflecting upon the miraculous deliverance of the three Jews, the king has been persuaded of the sovereignty of this delivering god.[3]

Nebuchadnezzar, the Pious Narrator: Verse 4 [1]

Nebuchadnezzar ends his doxology only to assume the role of narrator. As he begins his narrative (vs. 4 [1]), we realize that something other than the incident involving Shadrach, Meshach, and Abednego has brought about his conversion. The story we are about to hear will explain the king's song of praise to the Most High. Hence, we enter the story at the end. The pagan king is now a convert to the worship of the Most High. The distortion of the natural chronological order of the story's events effectively catches and retains our curiosity. We see the story's outcome, but do not know what has brought it about. We read on to piece together the puzzle of the past.

Nebuchadnezzar presents himself as a mediator, a spokesperson for the Most High. His purpose is to "disclose the signs and wonders of the Most High." The word "disclose" (*hawah*) occurred frequently in chapter 2, we may recall. There what was disclosed was the dream and its interpretation, that is, the message and intention of the Most High.

There only Daniel could disclose this knowledge of God. Here in chapter 4 when Nebuchadnezzar uses the same word in a similar context we may suspect that he, too, is implicitly claiming power to reveal special knowledge of God. Nebuchadnezzar and Daniel, formerly opponents, are now being focused more closely together.

The phrase "signs and wonders" usually refers specifically to acts or events that embody a communication from God, mostly to YHWH's deeds in bringing Israel out of slavery in Egypt (Exod 7:13; Deut 4:34; 6:22; etc.), in others to activities of prophetic mediation (Deut 13:1-2; Isa 8:18; 20:3). By appropriating this language, Nebuchadnezzar, whether consciously or not, elevates his role of mediator, one who imparts divine knowledge to his people. His authority is derived (apart from his kingship) from the experience he is about to relate, an experience that his language equates with Israel's exodus from Egypt.

Nebuchadnezzar's portrayal of himself as an authority on the Most High, as a spokesperson for this god whom he did not even recognize in chapter 1, is more than a little ironic. How he identifies the "Most High"—whether as the god of the Jerusalem temple, the god of Daniel, or the god of Shadrach, Meshach, and Abednego—is at this point unclear. Nevertheless, the reader knows that this is indeed one and the same god—and here is this king, who has destroyed this god's house and has exiled this god's people, speaking now as this god's chosen representative! Such unmitigated gall might well elicit a reader's hostility. Alternatively, we might suspect that the king is at the mercy of a hidden, implied narrator (a narrator behind the narrator, so to speak), and so see a touch of humor in the absurdity of the situation.

Curiosity lures us into Nebuchadnezzar's story. Such a pious testimonial from this persecutor of the god of the Jews? How has this conversion come about? After the doxology, the king begins to answer.

A Troubling Dream: Verses 5-17 [2-14]

He takes us back into his past. He recalls an earlier time of contentment and prosperity. A dream, however, brings fear and alarm:

> "I, Nebuchadnezzar, was content in my house and was flourishing in my palace. I had a dream and it made me afraid. While I was upon my couch, the imaginings[4] and the visions of my head troubled me . . . ." (4:4-5 [1-2])

Discontent's onset is important for a conversion story. Contented people are not easy converts. Trouble's intrusion into self-contentment here foreshadows, moreover, later disclosures, in particular the king's expulsion (vss. 29-33 [26-30]). The troubling dream also looks back to chapter 2. Nebuchadnezzar, it seems, is developing a history of nightmares. The reader might very well ask, has this dream anything to do with that earlier dream?

At least we surmise that the dream has had something to do with the royal narrator's conversion. It is perhaps the key to his change. What is this dream?, we wonder. But we must continue to wonder, because, rather than divulge it to us now, at the point in his story where he dreamed it (cf. Pharaoh's dreams in Genesis 41), he waits.

He summons his sages (vs. 6 [3]) and we again see phantoms of chapter 2. We are not surprised, then, at the sages' inability to explain the dream nor are we surprised when Daniel comes to the king's assistance. Unlike chapter 2, however, the king's request for interpretation (vs. 7 [4]) is not absurdly difficult or charged with tension. No one is threatened for failure; no one is accused of treason. When Daniel arrives (vs. 8 [5]), the king's expression of confidence in Daniel's ability is so strong (vs. 9 [9]) that the reader can hardly doubt that Daniel will interpret the dream. Even though Daniel's ability is contrasted to the inability of the sages, this competitive element is not magnified. The story is not a story about court contest, but centers on a particular experience of the main character, Nebuchadnezzar the king.

Daniel comes before the king as Belteshazzar, the name given to him by the Babylonian administration. This name, the king observes, reflects the name of the king's god. The king first tells us, and then tells Daniel, that he knows that "the spirit of the holy gods" is in him. Nebuchadnezzar's impression of Daniel, established at the end of chapter 2, appears not to have changed. To him, Daniel is still a curious mixture of human and divine, a sage with an awe-inspiring ability to solve any mystery.

Daniel's presence now provides the king his chosen opportunity to tell us what he has dreamed (vss. 10-17 [7-14].

In his dream, the king sees a great tree extending over all the earth, nourishing and protecting all the animals. Then, a "watcher" or "wakeful one" descends from heaven and commands that the tree be felled, leaving only the stump. The watcher instructs further that the heart of the tree be changed from that of a human to that of a beast and that this transformation remain until "seven times" have passed.

The dream does not divulge the recipients of these instructions. We never know who is to fell, bind, and transform the tree. We are told, however, that these events are a communication to the "living":

> "By the decree of the watching ones is the sentence and by the word of the holy ones is the command in order that the living will know that the Most High rules in the human kingdom and to whomever he pleases he gives it and the lowest of persons he sets over it." (4:17 [14])

To whom does "the living" refer? The breadth of the term, like "all peoples, nations, and languages who dwell in all the earth," may keep us aware that this communication has several dimensions. The living most obviously refers to the dreamer (as he exists in the story world), but the term also includes the internal audience presumed in the story world, as well as the external audience (the "implied reader").

The great tree condemned by a holy one is strongly reminiscent of the great image shattered by the divine stone in the king's earlier dream. Might we safely guess, in this instance, that the great tree, like the head of gold, is none other than Nebuchadnezzar? The king himself anticipates this association when he begins, "I was content in my house, flourishing in my palace." The word *ra‹anan*, "flourishing," is almost always used of plants, either literally or metaphorically.[5]

Prophetic tradition, where the image of the great tree is popular, also invites us to associate the tree with the king. The prophets use the image of the great tree to describe and usually indict political entities. On the one hand, the image has positive connotations. It is symbolic of messianic rule (for example, Isa 11:1-3, 10; Ezek 17:22-24; Hosea 14:5-7). On the other hand, the Hebrew prophets also use the image to pass judgment on the pride of political power (Isa 10:33-34; Ezek 31:1-12).

A Message from God

Just as the preceding oracles represent God's point of view, so, we might assume, does this dream. Nebuchadnezzar's earlier dream in chapter 2 was, after all, a message from God. But if the tree is the vehicle through which God sees him, then this image itself suggests that the relationship between God and the king is indeed ambiguous.

On the one hand, God must view Nebuchadnezzar as an agent, a protector and nourisher of all living things. Like the trees in Eden (which Ezekiel 31 suggests we compare) and particularly the tree of life, the tree in the dream provides food and shelter. On the other hand, God must also view Nebuchadnezzar as an enemy, a mortal who, like the tree, reaches to heaven. Heaven represents God (vs. 26 [23]). The dream, then, portrays the king as one who grasps divinity for himself. Just as, in the Eden story, the tree of knowledge of good and evil represents the human desire to know all, that is, to be like God, so, too, the tree in the dream is representative of a human being wanting to be like a god (Heaton, 149; Hartman, 78-79; DiLella, 255-258). The dream implies that he considers himself above humanity, a tree of life nourishing the whole world. The existence of the entire world depends upon him. He acknowledges no other source of power besides himself. This is the sin for which he is to be punished.

As a message of divine judgment, the dream is remarkably like our synchronic reading of the dream in chapter 2. In that earlier dream, the image symbolizing human pride, accomplishment, and power is brought down by divine fiat. In this dream, the tree reaching heaven is to be hewn down by the order of the holy ones. The resemblance of this dream to the former one raises a question: If the dream embodies a message from God, why is Nebuchadnezzar being sent another dream so like the first?

Why must the king be shown the impending divine judgment again? Perhaps because he did not perceive it the first time. We know from his failure to display any signs of repentance that he does not understand the earlier dream to be a judgment against him personally. On the contrary, he is so enraptured with the idea of his being the gold head of a gigantic image that he immediately constructs (in chapter 3) a gigantic gold image that symbolizes his power. Why does he interpret the earlier dream to be a personal confirmation rather than a personal indictment? Could it be because Daniel only explains the temporal dimensions of that dream and portrays it only as a vision of posthumous events. Because Daniel does not tell the whole truth of the earlier dream, God must repeat the message.

Given this reading of the overarching story, then, our interest will also revolve around what Daniel will say about the dream this time.

Nebuchadnezzar's lack of perception is symbolized in the ironic contrast between the king and God's representative in the dream. The one descending from heaven is a "wakeful one" who sees the king's shortcomings, knows what is to become of him, and has the power to bring this about. The wakeful one stands in opposition to a "sleeping" Nebuchadnezzar who does not recognize his sin, does not know what the dream means, and has no power to keep it from coming about. One might say that the "watcher" has been keeping track of the king, has seen Daniel's failure to announce explicitly the judgment of the earlier dream, and now utters the judgment himself.

Daniel's Response:
Verses 18-19 [15-16]

Upon hearing the dream and Nebuchadnezzar's reiterated demand that he tell its interpretation (vs. 18 [15]), Daniel is taken aback and troubled (vs. 19 [16]). With this glimpse of the inner Daniel the reader should begin to recognize a narrative voice other than that of Nebuchadnezzar. The next sentence, referring to the king in the third person ("The king said"), confirms the presence of this external narrator. The shift in narrator, however, does not seem to disturb readers unduly. Many people upon a first reading do not realize that the shift has taken place.[6] It is a subtle shift: Though the first person ("I") becomes the third person ("the king/he"), the perceptual point of view remains the same—at least for the time being. We still see the events from Nebuchadnezzar's perspective, as the use of the name Belteshazzar in reference to Daniel confirms. As far as Nebuchadnezzar is concerned, he is addressing the sage Belteshazzar (not Daniel). Likewise when the sage responds (vs. 19 [16]), he speaks as Belteshazzar, just as Nebuchadnezzar would have perceived him.[7]

Thus it happens that in verse 19 the external narrator (whose presence we may have suspected since Nebuchadnezzar's absurdly pious doxology) joins the internal narrator (the king) in the telling of the story. The external and internal narrators balance the external and internal audiences and thus the process of communication is further complicated. Just as we realized earlier that Nebuchadnezzar's message to his subjects is not exactly the same as his message to us, now we become aware that the external narrator's message to us may not be the same as that of Nebuchadnezzar to us. In other words, the two narrators are not necessarily expressing the same point of view.

The interchange here between Daniel and Nebuchadnezzar differs from what takes place in chapter 2. When the king expresses his overwhelming confidence in Daniel, twice asserting that Daniel is of divine spirit (vss. 9 [6] and 18 [15]), Daniel says nothing to modify the king's understanding. He issues no disclaimers, as he does in chapter 2, that mysteries are revealed not by his own wisdom but by God in heaven. Nor does he need to consult the God of heaven for his answers as he does earlier. In this story Daniel knows the "mind" of God. He knows instantly what God means by the dream. In short, his behavior in this scene simply ingrains the king's earlier misunderstanding about Daniel's human status: Daniel conveniently allows the boundary between divine and human ability to remain blurred.[8]

His role as mediator between God and Nebuchadnezzar places him in a delicate position. It is clear that, as soon as he hears the king's account of the dream, he knows (as well as we do) that it is a decree of judgment from God. We are told that Daniel "was taken aback for a moment and his thoughts troubled him" (vs. 19 [16]). He is hesitant to say what the dream means, possibly because he fears to be the bearer of ill tidings, or possibly because he truly likes the king and is sorry to know what is about to befall him. Encouraged to speak by the king, he responds with "My lord, may the dream be for those who hate you and its interpretation for your enemies!" Whether this is a heartfelt exclamation or simply safe protocol preparing the king for bad news, the statement communicates that what he is about to tell Nebuchadnezzar is not something that he himself would wish upon him. In other words, Daniel disengages himself from God's message by his gentle protest that the Nebuchadnezzar's enemies, not the king himself, deserve the coming reprimand.

Daniel's Interpretation: Verses 20-27 [17-24]

Daniel says what we have surmised all along, that the dream is a decree of the Most High (vs. 24 [21]). As he proceeds with the interpretation, he repeats the dream with subtle but significant variations. He refers to the command to hew down the tree, but omits the watcher's elaboration: "Cut off its branches. Strip off its foliage and scatter its fruit. Let the beasts flee from beneath it and the birds from its branches" (vs. 14 [11]). Daniel thus avoids speaking of the complete loss of integrity, power, and influence that the king is to experience.

When Daniel recounts the next portion of the dream, he explains that the king will, for seven "times," live in the wild as the beasts do (vss. 24-25 [21-22]). He does not tell him that his "heart" will change from that of a human to that of an animal. Thus he fails to communicate the extent of the humiliation that is in store for the king.

He reiterates the reason for the divine decree (vs. 25 [22]). In the watcher's words, it is "in order that the living will know that the Most High rules in the human kingdom and to whomever he pleases he gives it and the lowest of persons he sets over it" (vs. 17 [14]). But Daniel changes "the living" to "you," making the decree appear to be strictly a personal issue between the Most High and the king and thus deflecting the point of the public nature of the king's humiliation. He also leaves out the phrase, "and the lowest of persons he sets over it [that is, the human kingdom]." Aware, perhaps, that the king could easily mistake the opinion of the Most High for that of Daniel himself, he carefully avoids calling him "the lowest of persons" to his face.

As he concludes his interpretation, he does not end his explanation as the dream itself ends, with the reason for divine judgment. Instead, he returns to the image of the stump left in the ground, the sole element of hope in the dream. That stump, he assures the king, means that his power will be returned to him when he has learned his lesson. In other words, the dream is not a message of utter destruction. The kingdom will be restored.

Daniel's selectivity in his interpretation adds up to a substantial softening of the divine decree as it might readily have been interpreted. In this sense, his interpretation here is like his interpretation in chapter 2: He tells the truth but not the whole truth. Why does he soften the judgment? Certainly, his is a precarious position as the messenger of doom. However, the choice to ameliorate the message might also have something to do with a conflict of interest. If Daniel's words in verse 19 [16]) are at all sincere, then clearly he does not wish to see the dream come to pass. After all, what becomes of Daniel if the king who favors him so strongly falls from power? His concluding advice to the king fits well this line of thought. He urges him to act to keep the divine judgment from coming about: "Break off your sins by doing righteousness, and your evil by showing favor to the oppressed. Perhaps there will be a lengthening of your contentment" (vs. 27 [24]).

We are neither told nor shown Nebuchadnezzar's immediate response to Daniel's interpretation or to his counsel to repent. Perhaps

Nebuchadnezzar, like the reader, is still a little unclear as to what "doing righteousness" and "showing favor to the oppressed" has to do with "knowing that heaven rules." While Daniel may be making some implicit connection between recognizing God's sovereignty and "doing what the Lord requires," the connection would seem to be quite lost on this pagan king who knows nothing of what this god requires. After all, neither the dream nor Daniel's interpretation of it has said anything specific about being sinful, unrighteous, evil, or oppressive—the dream seems to be centered around the king's recognizing the sovereignty of the Most High.

Thus the interchange between Daniel and Nebuchadnezzar abruptly closes with Daniel's advice.

The Judgment:
Verses 28-33 [25-30]

What we hear next is the foreshadowing summary: "All of this came upon Nebuchadnezzar the king." The narrator then jumps us a year beyond the time of the interchange. What Nebuchadnezzar has done in the interval is not told.

At the end of the year, the king walks atop his palace and utters the words that precipitate his doom: "Is this not great Babylon, which I have built as a royal house by my mighty power and for the honor of my majesty?" (vs. 30 [27]). The words of praise with which he intends to praise himself are heard in heaven as the words which condemn him.[9] As he claims the kingdom to be symbolic of his own glory, the voice from heaven declares the kingdom to be lost, the glory to be taken away. Repeated now for the third time, the divine sentence makes no mention this time of the great tree shading the earth or the stump that is to be left. The word is one of unqualified judgment.

It is rather ironic that Daniel suggests to the king that the Most High will respond to a change in *behavior* (vs. 27 [24]) whereas this episode implies that *words* trigger divine response. The correlation between speech and action is never quite spelled out in this story. The seeming priority of affective speech makes the earlier testimony of Nebuchadnezzar, in this reader's mind, suspect. Has Nebuchadnezzar found that simply the right words will appease the divine?

Nebuchadnezzar's speech atop his palace exposes to us the attitude imaged by the dream. Like the city builders in Genesis 11 (who, incidently, built in the same geographical location), Nebuchadnezzar has built his city Babylon (= Babel) for his own glory, in other words, to make a name for himself. The allusion to the tower of Babel underscores the dream's message of condemnation (cf. DiLella, 255-58; Knight, 441). The tree's height is reminiscent of the great tower. The tree, like the tower, reaches the heavens. The scattering of the peoples and the multiple languages that result from the building of the tower are reproduced in the dream when the fruit, the beasts, and the birds are scattered after the fall of the tree. The scattered ones in Nebuchadnezzar's world are the subjugated peoples, the peoples of many nations and languages to whom he addresses his correspondence.

The voice from heaven announces that Nebuchadnezzar, too, will be "scattered." He is to be driven from society and become like a beast for "seven times" until he "knows that the Most High rules in the human kingdom" (vss. 31-32 [28-29]). The judgment is immediately executed upon Nebuchadnezzar. Taken from the life of "flourishing" luxury, he is left, exposed to the natural elements, living and eating with and like the beasts (vs. 33 [30]).

Having at last confirmed to the reader, with this fourth report of the divine judgment, that judgment actually befell the king, the narrator elaborates on the man's bestial existence by adding: "His hair grew long like eagles' feathers and his nails like birds' claws" (vs. 33 [30]). Here we are told that the loss of societal contact and of mental faculties takes its toll physically. Rather than being like the great tree in the dream, Nebuchadnezzar takes on the characteristics of the dream's representations of his subjects—the birds and the beasts. He now acts like an ox and looks like bird. This final repetition of the decree caps the theme of poetic justice: A man who thinks he is like a god must become a beast to learn that he is only a human being.[10]

At last we know what has brought about the king's new-found piety. The power of the Most High has made its mark on him personally. The king has not witnessed the divine power in relation to someone else—that is, in Daniel's ability or in the deliverance of Shadrach, Meshach, and Abednego—but he has experienced this power himself.[11]

With another jump in time, implicitly spanning "seven times," the narrative resumes, but once again it is under the the king's direction: "At the end of the days, I, Nebuchadnezzar, lifted my eyes to heaven and my reason returned to me and I blessed the Most High and I praised and I glorified the one living forever . . ." (vs. 34 [31]).

The Narrators

Now that we have returned to the first-person narrator, it might be helpful to backtrack and consider carefully how this story is being told, especially since its combination of first-person narration and extensive flashback (obviously related devices) is unusual in biblical narrative.[12]

We have found a complex mixture of narrative voices. The first-person narration by the king about himself frames a substantial portion of third-person narration about him by another narrator. It would appear at first sight, therefore, that whatever is told in this middle portion of the story is controlled by Nebuchadnezzar; that is, he allows this material to be part of his proclamation to the world. When one steps back and considers chapter 4 in the context of the larger story in the book, however, another level of narration is evident. The third-person, implied narrator of the book controls the voice of Nebuchadnezzar. This narrator allows Nebuchadnezzar to tell part of his story, but does not allow him to tell all. The question then becomes, *Why* is Nebuchadnezzar not allowed to tell all? Before we can answer this question, however, an examination of the story's structure is in order.

Shaping the Story

Daniel 4 has been viewed by William Shea (202) as a chiastic pattern of form and content:[13]

Prologue: vss. 1-3
    Post-fulfillment proclamation
    Poem I
A vss. 4-7 Dream reception
    X vss. 8-9 Dialogue I—King to Daniel
        B vss. 10-17 Dream recital
            Y Dialogue II
                vs. 18-19a King to Daniel
                vs. 19b Daniel to King
        B' vss. 20-26 Dream interpretation
    Z vs. 27 Dialogue III—Daniel to King
A' vss. 28-33 Dream fulfillment
Epilogue: vss. 34-38
    Post-fulfillment restoration
    Poem II

How might recognition of this structure (which has been slightly modified) help a reader construe the story's meaning(s)? Shea invites us, without pursuing the matter, to consider associating certain parts of the story other than simply sequentially. So let us consider for a moment what effect some of these associations may have upon a reader.

Often the central point in a chiasm, here represented by **Y**, will indicate some sort of turning point in the story. Shea's designation of this center point is based on its formal characteristic, namely that it is dialogue. But what is taking place, what is being communicated, in this dialogue? Obviously, **Y** does not contain a plot climax (that comes in vss. 29-33 [26-30]), but something else important is happening at this point. It is precisely in the apex of the chiasm that a major shift in narrative voice, or narrative point of view, occurs. It is at this place in the story (with verse 19a) where the first-person narration of Nebuchadnezzar is taken over by a third-person narrator. The second half of the flashback (**B'**, **Z**, **A'**), then, represents a different point of view than that expressed by the original narrator, that is, Nebuchadnezzar.

Why the Third-Person Narrator?

What is the effect of having the implied narrator (that is, the third-person narrator) unveiled at point **Y**? To begin with, having this narrator report Daniel's interpretation of the dream reinforces our impression that Daniel's knowledge and wisdom are exclusive to him. The presence of this narrator emphasizes that there is no way Nebuchadnezzar could have access to Daniel's knowledge and wisdom except that he be told. Furthermore, by allowing Daniel's speech to stand on its own (rather than being quoted by the king), the third-person narrator sets Daniel's variation of the dream (**B'**) against Nebuchadnezzar's recitation of the dream (**B**). If Daniel's version of judgment is, as has been argued, softer than the dream's, then we can be assured that this diluted version is Daniel's doing and not the king's.

The control of the third-person narrator allows us to recognize that Nebuchadnezzar's point of view remains limited. Just as Daniel's interpretation (**B'**) presents a slightly different version of the dream (**B**), so Daniel's encouragement to repent (**Z**) represents a different view of the king's life than the view that the king himself has held (**X**). The Nebuchadnezzar of the pre-humiliation past has, to hear him tell it, no concept of himself as unrighteous, sinful, evil, or oppressive. For Nebuchadnezzar, the dream comes at an arbitrary moment, while he is "flourishing," content in his home. The untimely dream is a mystery to be solved by someone in whom is the "spirit of the holy gods." Daniel, however, views the king's lifestyle to be in need of correction.

This question of reliability requires that the events subsequent to Daniel's interpretation also be told by the implied narrator. Given Nebuchadnezzar's proud speech, his desire to see himself in the most glorious light possible, we would have difficulty in accepting his version of the words of condemnation were the telling to be his. Even more problematic would be his own account of his subsequent downfall: A madman is prone to make an unreliable narrator. The voice of the third-person narrator, then, confirms the mental incompetence of the beast-like king. The king is an unreliable witness of these events. Moreover, the account is "protected" from the self-interests of Nebuchadnezzar who, even after regaining his sanity, might not want to portray himself in such a humiliating light.

There is, finally, an inherent irony in the third-person narrator's control. Nebuchadnezzar may think himself sovereign of the world, but he is not even sovereign of his own story. This powerful king who has conquered the world needs a little help recounting his experience. Just as the dream (as well as Daniel's explanation) is intended to help him see himself more clearly, so the third-person narration helps him to get his story straight, helps him to remember what he may not want to remember, and forces him to tell his audiences what has happened, including details which he may not want them to know.

Another Doxology: Verses 34-35 [31-32]

When Nebuchadnezzar regains his reason, he is allowed to resume his story. Now that he is mentally competent, he can continue.

> At the end of the days, I, Nebuchadnezzar, lifted my eyes to heaven and my reason returned to me and I blessed the Most High and I praised and I glorified the one living forever. (4:34a [31a])

At this point his speech breaks into another doxology:

> His rule is an everlasting rule
>   and his kingdom is with generation after generation.
> All the inhabitants of the earth are accounted as nothing
>   and he does as he pleases in the host of heaven

and among the inhabitants of the earth.
There is no one who hinders his hand
or says to him "What are you doing?" (4:34b-35 [31b-32])

Whether these are his words of blessing, offered as he looks to heaven, or subsequent words, is unclear. Whatever the case, they are followed by his comment: "In that moment my reason returned to me" (vs. 36a [33a]). Thus his blessing, praise, and glorification of the Most High are framed by the phrase, "my reason returned to me." The placing of this phrase both before and after the praising makes the precise chronology of events uncertain. Does his reason return *before* he praises the Most High or does his reason return *after*, that is, *as a result of*, his words of praise.

The voice from heaven has implied that acknowledgment of God's sovereignty will bring an end to his punishment. Is God simply responding favorably to the king's declaration of divine praise, just as God responded unfavorably to the king's declaration of self-praise?

Granted, Nebuchadnezzar has not only discovered the appropriate thing to say to the Most High, he has also learned how to say it. From Israel's own religious language (cf. Psalm 145:10-13), language designed to bend God's ear and effect God's response, he has constructed his doxology. Should we construe the ease in which the words trip off his tongue to be evidence of genuine piety? Or should his smooth, cultically correct language be cause to suspect his sincerity?

In any event the *words*, like those spoken on the rooftop, evoke divine response. God's preoccupation with human speech is cast in a rather ironic light. Is God satisfied with the words because of their pious trappings? Is God satisfied with an acknowledgment of divine sovereignty even when it comes from a madman? If the madman is Nebuchadnezzar, king of "all peoples, nations and languages," God is satisfied with verbal acknowledgment. Because, in order for "the living" (that is, the audiences both inside and outside the story) to know that the Most High rules in the human kingdom," "the living" must hear the human king say so.

The Glory of Rule: Verse 36 [33]

Nebuchadnezzar concludes his flashback with an account of his re-establishment upon the throne:

> In that moment my reason returned to me and, for the glory of my kingdom, my majesty and my splendor returned to me. My counselors and my lords sought me and I was established over my kingdom and exceeding greatness was added to me. (4:36 [33])

In speaking of his restoration, his pious language disappears, at least temporarily. Here even the content of his speech betrays him. No longer does he speak of God's rule, God's kingdom, or the greatness of God's signs and wonders. Instead he speaks of "the *glory* of *my* kingdom," "*my majesty* and *my splendor*," "*my* exceeding *greatness*." There is no word about God's part in his restoration. In fact, the words are reminiscent of the very speech that caused his downfall: "Is this not *great* Babylon, which I have built as a royal house by *my* mighty power and for the *glory* of *my majesty*?" As far as he is concerned—"exceeding greatness was added to me"—he is greater than ever before.

Listening to Nebuchadnezzar's words, we realize that we have heard many of them before in this chapter. In his first doxology (vs. 3 [3:33]), Nebuchadnezzar speaks of how "great" and "mighty" are the signs and wonders of the Most High God. The next few times these words appear (vss. 11, 20, 22 [8, 17, 19]) they describe the great tree that represents Nebuchadnezzar. They then appear in subsequent speeches of the king. First, "Is this not *great* Babylon which I have built as a royal house by my *mighty* power . . . ?" Finally, when his ordeal is over, he reports his restoration: ". . . for the glory of my kingdom, my honor and my splendor returned to me . . . and exceeding *greatness* was added to me." "Exceeding greatness" is "added" to what Daniel describes as a greatness that already "reaches the heavens" (vs. 22 [19]). The words that are used to describe God are the same words used to describe Nebuchadnezzar in the dream, in Daniel's speech and in the speeches of the king himself (Towner 1984:59). Not only does the king praise himself with the same terms that he uses to praise God, but his self-praise grows even more strident at the end. He cannot completely break away from his sin of hubris.

Other often repeated words that apply to both human and divine sovereign are words of political control: "rule," "king," and "kingdom." Who rules in the human kingdom? This question is indeed the heart of the story.

In his opening doxology Nebuchadnezzar says of the Most High God, "His kingdom is an everlasting kingdom and his rule is with generation after generation" (4:3 [3:33]). But, as we have seen, the king has not always been of this persuasion. Daniel's interpretation of the dream implies that both the king and his subjects have perceived the king to be in command: "It is you, O King, who have grown great and mighty. Your greatness has grown and reaches to the heavens and your rule to the end of the earth" (vs. 22 [19]). The decree from heaven has been issued in order that everyone may learn otherwise, that "the Most High rules in the human kingdom and to whomever he pleases he gives it" (vss. 17, 25, 26, 32 [14, 22, 23, 29]).

When Nebuchadnezzar acknowledges this divine sovereignty, his kingdom is given back as promised. He declares at the end, in a slight rearrangement of his opening doxology: "His rule is an everlasting rule and his kingdom is with generation after generation" (vs. 34 [31]). When Nebuchadnezzar recognizes the kingdom of the Most High, his own kingdom is restored to him with more glory and splendor than before. When he acknowledges the Most High as the "King of heaven" (vs. 37 [34]), he himself is restored to kingship and "exceeding greatness is added" to him.

Does Nebuchadnezzar perceive that there is a kinship among kings? Yes, says the language that overlaps human and divine sovereignty. Mary Daly (19) has pointed out the danger of using singular models for God: "If God is male, then the male is God." The same principle applies in this character's perception. If "greatness," "might," "kingdom," and "rule" are the kingly attributes of God, then these attributes, when applied to a human being, become godly. If God is king, then the king is God. Whether the association is conscious or unconscious on the part of Nebuchadnezzar, he somehow connects God's glory and power with his own. Thus the acknowledgement of sovereignty has come full circle.

Pious Words: Verse 37 [34]

When he jumps back to the present (vs. 37 [34]) he resumes his pious language, but he chooses his words carefully: "Now, I, Nebuchadnezzar, praise and extol and glorify the king of heaven for all his works are right and his ways are just . . . ." He does not repeat the words of the watcher: "the Most High rules in the human kingdom . . . and the lowest of persons he sets over it" (vs. 17 [14]). Instead Nebuchadnezzar talks of God's ability to bring down "those walking in pride" or perhaps "those walking in majesty"—the meaning of the term is somewhat ambiguous. The point is that Nebuchadnezzar is impressed with God's ability to bring "down" those who are "high." He certainly does not want to be brought down again. Consequently, his pious language might be seen as insurance against this happening. This is not to suggest that he is taking the divine display of power lightly. Quite the contrary, nothing impresses those with power like those with more power. But if pious language is what it takes to keep this powerful god at bay (and to keep the human king himself in a position of sovereignty), then pious language is what this god will get. And the reader asks, Who is ruling whom?

So, what is the reader to make of this pious testimony of the king who destroyed Jerusalem and its temple and exiled its people? He has said the right words in the right way. Does he convince us that he recognizes divine sovereignty? Does he convince the God of heaven, for that matter? Or, in the words of Qoheleth 8:4, does the word of the king rule after all? Does Nebuchadnezzar control the "signs and wonders" of God by commanding the attention of the world? Does he not leave us with a vision that blurs "the glory of my kingdom" with the "everlasting kingdom" of the Most High?

The Dead King

But Qoheleth also reminds us: "there is no rule in the day of death." Eventually, "the wicked are buried" (Eccl 8:8, 10). This is an ironic comment indeed on the voice of the dead king in Daniel 4. As we listen to Nebuchadnezzar's voice from the grave, we are reminded that, eventually, all oppressors are brought down, not just temporarily, but ultimately. And so it is in this story: In the storyteller's world, the fate of Nebuchadnezzar is left unspoken and yet is abruptly disclosed. When Nebuchadnezzar closes his testimonial, there is no coda. The next sentence is the first sentence of the story that follows: King Belshazzar made a great feast . . ." (5:1). Somewhere between the ending of chapter 4 and the beginning of chapter 5, Nebuchadnezzar is no more. (And we might wonder if the God of heaven is uncomfortable with the king's ambiguous testimony after all.)

Perhaps the most ironic aspect of this extraordinary next sentence lies in the reader's realization that Nebuchadnezzar says, or is made to say, in death what the historical Nebuchadnezzar never would have said in life.[14] He is made to utter praise (however ambiguous) for a god for whom the historical king had no respect. In its confrontation with the historical Nebuchadnezzar, the Israelite community was impotent. But years later a member of this once impotent community played a joke on the infamous king of the exile by creating a new memory of Nebuchadnezzar, a memory of which the historical king would have never approved. In the minds of most readers, the new memory no doubt overshadows the old. And thus we see what the author of this story must have known, that the human imagination is able to overpower human history.[15]

Chapter Five

DANIEL 5

YOUR FATHER THE KING

Belshazzar's Feast:
Verses 1-4

The beginning is abrupt: "King Belshazzar made a great feast . . . ." The reader must immediately come to attention, struggle to get bearings. The action begins before we know who Belshazzar is, when this is happening, why he is giving a feast, or what has happened to the character who has been king up to this point—Nebuchadnezzar. Such an abrupt start may remind us of the earlier, equally impulsive beginning of chapter 3, "King Nebuchadnezzar made an image of gold . . . ." As on that occasion, we are given few directions—no temporal clause to ease us into the story, as in chapters 1 and 2, no epistolary formula to orient us to the narrator and narrative, as in chapter 4.

Once we associate the opening phrases of chapters 5 and 3, we may notice that more connects them than just the fact that they are both disjointed beginnings. They duplicate grammar as well as vocabulary: "Belshazzar *the king made* . . . " parallels "Nebuchadnezzar *the king made* . . . ." One makes a great feast, the other a great image.

This striking similarity raises the question: Are the sentences similar in function? Obviously both establish the context of the subsequent events, but do they do more than that? In discussing chapter 3 we noted that its opening sentence reports the strategic event that initiates the plot. The image becomes the element around which conflict ensues. Does the opening sentence of chapter 5 function the same way? Perhaps Belshazzar's feast is not simply the setting of the story, but something more significant. We shall come back to this point.

A further similarity between the sentences is that both develop a description of excess. Nebuchadnezzar builds an image "of gold whose height was sixty cubits and its width six cubits." Belshazzar makes the feast "for a thousand of his lords and he drank wine in front of the thousand." But by now we may be noticing that the parallels between beginnings run beyond these first sentences. Once the image is erected, Nebuchadnezzar demands the assembly of a whole cast of political officials for the dedication of the image. Repeating the instruction word for word, even the list of officials, the narrator reports that the king's demand is fulfilled (3:2-3). In similar fashion, once Belshazzar inaugurates the feast, he commands that the vessels from the Jerusalem temple be brought in order that he and his guests can drink from them. The narrator reports that this is carried out exactly as commanded and, as the narrator does in Daniel 3, even repeats the list of the guests who are present (5:2-3). Furthermore, it is at this point in both stories that the people assembled pay homage to idols (3:4-7; 5:4).

These similarities, then, invite us to consider the earlier story as we read the new one. They occur where we are most plagued by gaps in our knowledge: Who is Belshazzar and what has he to do with Nebuchadnezzar? What is the nature and purpose of this feast? Why does he send specifically for the Jerusalem temple vessels? Chapter 3 can aid us in filling these gaps if we recognize the presence of its shadow from the beginning of our reading of chapter 5.

Hence, as we begin our reading, two characters and their actions are paired: Belshazzar and Nebuchadnezzar. Both are kings. Both "make" grand things. Both invite a multitude of subjects to admire and/or participate in these things. The story's second sentence gives us important information that formally links the two kings: "When he tasted the wine, Belshazzar commanded that the vessels of gold and silver that Nebuchadnezzar his father had taken from the temple in Jerusalem be brought . . . ." Thus we learn that the two kings are not simply being paired; they fall into a chronological pattern. One comes after the other. One knows of the other and imitates. A son models his father.

So, what was his father doing in chapter 3? Nebuchadnezzar's golden image, it was argued, represented his attempt to insure political and religious unity in his kingdom. His requirement that all his officials pay homage to the image was a symbolic demand that they swear complete political allegiance to him.

What then of Belshazzar's feast? Does it not serve the same function? Is it not like Adonijah's feast in 1 Kings 1, a feast designed to allure the political allegiance of subjects and to consolidate political power?

However, lest we conclude too quickly "like father, like son," consider how the two differ. The focus of Nebuchadnezzar's assembly is the image that he made. Whatever the image stands for, the accent falls on the fact that it is the king's accomplishment—and appropriately so, for Nebuchadnezzar has achieved political power through accomplishment.[1] Belshazzar, on the other hand, has accomplished nothing significant as far as we know. The focus of his assembly is himself. He centers attention upon himself by "drinking wine in front of the thousand." The narrator's language centers him: Everyone present is described in terms of him—*his* lords, *his* wives, *his* concubines.

The two kings handle their power in significantly different ways. Nebuchadnezzar commands his officials' allegiance with the threat of death; Belshazzar cajoles his lords with wine and merriment. Nebuchadnezzar assumes power; Belshazzar still needs affirmation of power. Consequently, Belshazzar is much like Adonijah son of David in 1 Kings 1.[2] Although Belshazzar already possesses the title of king while Adonijah has yet to secure it, the two characters are alike in that both must deal with the reputations of their fathers. Neither son has done anything to compare with the accomplishments of his father, yet each wants his father's power and position. They have done nothing to command respect and political support so they buy respect and support with food, wine, and entertainment by giving feasts to celebrate themselves.

The Temple Vessels

If Belshazzar has accomplished nothing worthy of note thus far, then perhaps the feast will provide the opportunity for him to confirm himself before his lords. And indeed, the feast does give him the chance to do something quite extraordinary:

> When he tasted the wine, Belshazzar commanded that the vessels of gold and silver that Nebuchadnezzar his father had taken from the temple in Jerusalem be brought and they, the king and his lords, his wives and his concubines, would drink wine from them. (5:2)

Why does he specify these particular vessels from the temple in Jerusalem? Has he simply always fancied them? Are they somehow grander, more ornate than other vessels, even other temple vessels? Is he at odds with the god to whom these belong and is he overtly defying this god? Is he equating vessels of gold and silver with gods of gold and silver[3] or does he consider himself merely to be using sacred things to serve sacred subjects, that is, the gods of gold and silver, bronze, iron, wood and stone?

A clue to an answer might be found in a comparison of Belshazzar's command (vs. 2) with the narrator's report of its fulfillment (vs. 3). The command concerns "the vessels which Nebuchadnezzar his father had taken from the temple in Jerusalem." The narrator's report describes the vessels as the "vessels that were taken from the temple which is the house of God that is in Jerusalem." The variances are subtle but significant. The two statements represent two different points of view. For Belshazzar, the importance of the vessels lies in the fact that *Nebuchadnezzar his father* had taken them. But, for the narrator (as also for the implied reader), the vessels are significant because they are from *the house of God* in Jerusalem.[4]

The reader's interest in the vessels—an interest which, in turn, may arouse a sense of foreboding—stems from an investment in "the god in Jerusalem." Belshazzar, however, has no such investment. He has no quarrel with the god of Jerusalem. He has no reason to try to prove that this god is a "phony" (Towner 1984:72). Nor does the text give us any indication that Belshazzar is trying "to reassure himself by degrading what frightens him" (Lacocque, 94). Belshazzar is a religious man. He worships all sorts of gods. If he is anxious to gain the favor of the gods of gold, silver, bronze, iron, wood and stone, why should he seek to offend any other god, particularly the god of Jerusalem?[5]

Belshazzar's motive lies in something else. He sends for the vessels which Nebuchadnezzar his father had captured. This allusion takes us back to the introduction of chapter 1, of chapters 1-6, of the book of Daniel as a whole. That opening reads:

> In the third year of the reign of Jehoiakim king of Judah, Nebuchadnezzar king of Babylon came to Jerusalem and besieged it. And Adonai gave Jehoiakim king of Judah into his hand, with some of the vessels of the house of God; and he brought them to the land of Shinar, to the house of his god, and he placed the vessels in the treasury of his god. (1:1-2)

When originally discussing this text, we noted the disparity between the narrator's point of view and Nebuchadnezzar's point of view concerning the conquest of Jerusalem. For Nebuchadnezzar, the capture of the city, its king, and its temple's vessels is the result of his military expertise and the support of his personal god. The narrator and the reader know, however, that Adonai has *given* to him the Judean king and the temple vessels. To Nebuchadnezzar, the vessels symbolize his success and, implicitly, the success of his god. He does not realize, as does the reader, that the vessels are a *gift* from the god to whom they belong.[6] Nevertheless, it is to his credit that he does realize the sacred nature of the vessels and he respects that sacredness by placing them in the treasury of his god.

We are now close to an understanding of why Belshazzar calls for the temple vessels. The argument runs along the following lines.

In the story world of Daniel (which is the nationally self-centered world of the Hebrew narrator), the capture of Jerusalem and its temple is portrayed as Nebuchadnezzar's major military conquest, despite the fact that he does not realize how this success came about. Granted, this conquest assumes such importance by default—it is the only one mentioned. Nonetheless, it is, for the narrator, Nebuchadnezzar's most noteworthy achievement. The temple vessels are the symbol of this success. For his part, Belshazzar, the son who has accomplished nothing, has to vie with the reputation of his father. He tries to show himself superior to his father as a means of gaining credibility in the eyes of his subjects.

One way to outdo his father is to take his father's accomplishments and values lightly.[7] Hence, he sends for the vessels, not because they belong to the god of Jerusalem, but because they represent his father's greatest deed. He belittles his father's achievement by using the vessels as if they were ordinary things.[8] He discredits his father's values by demonstrating that what his father considered sacred is not sacred to him. And he shows himself to be more courageous than his father by doing something his father would never do—drinking from a vessel dedicated to a god. And let us not forget, that although the vessels are from the house of God in Jerusalem, they have since been dedicated to *Nebuchadnezzar's* god. By drinking from these vessels, Belshazzar is saying, like Rehoboam, Solomon's son, in 1 Kings 12:10, "My little finger is thicker than my father's loins."

By telling us that Belshazzar sends for the vessels after he has drunk some wine[9] the narrator is not necessarily suggesting that the act is impulsive (cf. Anderson, 53). On the contrary, details of the text argue strongly that Belshazzar's act is premeditated. He knows exactly which vessels he wants and what he wants to do with them. The command is given before a thousand of his lords, not whispered to a butler. His act claims authority over Nebuchadnezzar his father; his act must be witnessed to have its desired effect.

Belshazzar's act is brash and the wine fortifies him to carry it through. This scene has its parallel. In 2 Samuel 16 Absalom has mounted a rebellion against his father and seized Jerusalem. When Absalom seeks counsel concerning what he should do next, he is told "Go in to your father's concubines, whom he has left to keep the house; and all Israel will hear that you have made yourself odious to your father, and the hands of all who are with you will be strengthened." The narrator reports that Absalom complied: "So they pitched a tent for Absalom upon the roof; and Absalom went in to his father's concubines in the sight of all Israel" (2 Sam 16:21-22). The word of his counsellor is all the encouragement Absalom needs. For Belshazzar, the wine is his encouragement. The wine steels him to do what he has decided to do; it is his "shot of courage." As Absalom profanes his father's concubines, Belshazzar profanes the vessels of his father's conquest, the vessels dedicated to his father's god.

Furthermore, just as both Absalom and Adonijah offer sacrifices as they claim the authority of kingship (cf. 2 Sam 15:7-12 and 1 Kgs 1:9, 19), so, too, Belshazzar invites divine blessing by offering praise (and perhaps wine also) to the gods of gold and silver, bronze, iron, wood, and stone. Such a list of deities suggests that Belshazzar is soliciting favor from seemingly every quarter.[10] Again political insecurity suggests itself as the driving force behind such excess.

The Writing on the Wall: Verses 5-9

"In that moment" the fingers of a human hand appear and write upon the palace wall (vs. 5). The narrator connects this next event to the preceding one, not causally but chronologically. The king sees the hand as it writes. The narrator then describes, in detail and not without touches of irony and humor, the visual effect this sight has upon the king:

> Then the king's color changed, his thoughts troubled him, the knots of his loins were loosened, and his knees knocked against each other. (5:6)

In chapters 2 and 4, after dreaming significant dreams, King Nebuchadnezzar, too, is afraid. In these stories the narrator describes the king as having a troubled spirit, being unable to sleep, or being troubled by the visions of his head. Never once does Nebuchadnezzar allow his fear to be manifested physically in public view. Belshazzar, on the other hand, loses his composure. He shows all the signs of being overcome by what he has just witnessed. His face pales, his knees knock and, depending upon how one understands the image "the knots of his loins were loosened," either his legs give way or he loses control of certain bodily functions (cf. Nahum 2:11). The man who would surpass Nebuchadnezzar is "turned to water" (cf. Ezek 7:17; 21:7 [12]). The king who would appear powerful shows himself to be weak.

As might be expected, the king now calls for the Babylonian sages. Even in this stereotypical reaction, however, the narrator's choice of words sustains a contrast between Belshazzar and Nebuchadnezzar. The latter, when he needs the sages, *commands* that they be called (2:2) and, on the second occasion, *issues a decree* to this effect (4:6 [3]). Although both times in a state of anxiety, he acts authoritatively. Belshazzar, on the other hand, *cries loudly* for sages to be brought (5:7). He responds in panic (cf. Driver, 63).

The contrasts continue. When Nebuchadnezzar summons his sages in chapter 2, he promises them reward for success, but only after he has threatened death for failure. He is an uncompromising king who uses his power as he wills. In chapter 4, the sages' performance as well as their appearance falls under the command of the king's decree (4:6 [3]). King Belshazzar, however, only promises reward, and rather excessive reward at that, to any sage who can explain the writing to him (5:7). Considering the task—at least there is visible writing on the wall; no one is required to recount someone else's dream—he acts with decidedly less assurance than does King Nebuchadnezzar.

When the royal sages fail to comply (which comes as no surprise to the audience), the king becomes even more troubled and his color changes further (vss. 8-9).

The Queen's Perspective: Verses 10-12

Upon hearing of the excitement at the banquet, the queen mother comes into the drinking hall to speak to the king (vs. 10).[11]

As Lacocque (97) has observed, the queen plays a role like that of Arioch in chapter 2. She brings Daniel to the attention of the king. The narrator also uses her to bring several important dimensions to the story. Notice her first words to the king: "O King, live forever! Do not let your thoughts trouble you or your color change" (vs. 10). Because her language echoes that of the narrator, the reader knows that, at least to some extent, her perception of the king's condition is correct. Her language, however, is double-edged. While on the one hand, her words *speak* a message of comfort, on the other hand, her words *function* to bring attention to the king's discomfort. If any of those present have missed the king's display of fear, she makes sure that they now take note of it.

She sees for herself, upon entering the room, what we have just been shown. However, her perception of the situation is not entirely complete. As she continues her speech, she tells the king of Daniel and expresses her confidence that he can show the interpretation. She never mentions the strange appearance of the hand or the actual event of the writing. She connects the king's anxiety strictly with the fact that the writing has not been interpreted. Her attitude is such that, once the writing is interpreted, the problem will be solved, the crisis will be over, the matter settled. She does not speculate on what the mystery has to do with the situation at hand or how the interpretation might affect the lives of the people involved.

The queen's speech also contributes to the story a detailed description of Daniel. Her speech allows us to see him from her point of view. Her impression of Daniel borders on hero worship: He has "the spirit of the holy gods," "illumination and insight and wisdom like the wisdom of the gods," "an excellent spirit and knowledge and an insight to interpret dreams and to disclose riddles and to solve problems" (vss. 11-12). Her words link Daniel with the divine. Some do this directly: he has "the spirit of the holy gods" and "wisdom like the wisdom of the gods." Others are indirect: he has "light" or "illumination," an attribute of God (cf. his thanksgiving in 2:22).

Her praise of his ability "to solve problems" may also set up interesting overtones. The phrase, which is literally "to loosen knots," connects Daniel's ability to solve problems with the "loosened knots" of the king. While we cannot be sure whether or not the queen is aware of her word play, we cannot help but wonder, at the suggestion of her words, if she has not only noted the color of the king's face, but also a puddle at his feet! The funny little word play foreshadows Daniel's ironic role in the story. If the hand writing on the wall has "loosened the knots of the king's loins," what does the queen think Daniel's interpretation will do? Does she suspect that Daniel will only increase the king's fear? She seems somewhat removed from the king's problem. Why that should be so remains to be seen.

An important aspect of the queen's characterization of Daniel has yet to be discussed. She connects him to the reign of Nebuchadnezzar. Daniel's abilities, she tells Belshazzar, were discovered "in the days of your father." And "King Nebuchadnezzar, your father," she continues, recognized his superior ability and "elevated him to chief of the magicians, enchanters, Chaldeans, and astrologers—*your father the king*."[12]

Again her language *does* more than it *says*. On the surface, she is communicating Daniel's credibility: She recommends him on the basis of his service to Nebuchadnezzar. However, by using the phrase "your father the king," the queen also communicates two kinds of hierarchy. Fathers command the respect of sons and kings command the respect of subjects. By referring to Nebuchadnezzar as "the king," she undermines Belshazzar's own title. That is to say, we might well hear her words implying that Nebuchadnezzar was a real king while Belshazzar has yet to prove himself. Furthermore, she tells Belshazzar that the king (that is, Nebuchadnezzar) gave Daniel the name Belteshazzar.[13] Not only is she informing Belshazzar that Daniel was highly regarded during the reign of Nebuchadnezzar, but by quoting Nebuchadnezzar's own words concerning "the spirit of the holy gods" being in Daniel (cf. 4:8, 9, 18 [5, 6, 15]), she communicates specifically Nebuchadnezzar's attitude toward Daniel. Indeed, she is the voice, and perhaps not such a welcome voice, of the dead king Nebuchadnezzar.

An Unknown Daniel?

From her speech it appears that the queen is introducing a person unknown to Belshazzar. As already noted, her function seems to be, like that of Arioch in chapter 2, to inform the king about a resource of which he is unaware. Some commentators have noticed the incongruity of this situation. How can Belshazzar not know of the sage who ranked so highly in his father's administration? Anderson (57) argues in essence that the author has disregarded the incongruity in the interests of using a literary motif whereby an unknown hero succeeds where known professionals fail. Telling the story this way "add[s] lustre to the cause being championed by the author." Lacocque (97), on the other hand, explains the problem in terms of Belshazzar's character: "As for the 'ignorance' of Daniel's existence professed by Belshazzar, it is part of his psychological 'block' and is in parallel with Exod. 1.8: 'Now there arose over Egypt a new king who did not (want to) know Joseph' . . . ."

Both of these comments are helpful but not entirely satisfactory. The introduction of an unknown hero is indeed a common plot motif, as can be seen earlier in chapter 2 as well as in the Joseph story (Genesis 37-50), and in the stories introducing Saul and David in 1 Samuel. The motif may well be at work here. Yet this explanation, by appeal to the mechanics of composition, still leaves the incongruity intact: It still does not make sense that Belshazzar is unfamiliar with his father's chief sage. Lacocque's explanation addresses the question of meaning directly. He suggests that Belshazzar does not want to be familiar with Daniel. This reading is intriguing, but before we try to reach some conclusion on this issue, we must read further.

The queen's last words are "Now let Daniel be called and he will disclose the interpretation" (vs. 12). Knowing our narrator's love for repetition, we might expect the narrator to report at this point something like "And so the king called for Daniel in order that he might disclose the interpretation." But, oddly enough, Belshazzar does not call for Daniel nor does he say anything in answer to the queen. Daniel is simply "brought" upon the queen's suggestion. The queen's enthusiasm sweeps the plot along at this point. Belshazzar has, for the moment, lost control. Daniel is brought without the king's bidding.

Belshazzar's Perspective: Verses 13-16

When Belshazzar speaks to Daniel, he repeats much of what has happened thus far as well as part of what the queen has said. Repetitions and their variations often reveal surprising dimensions to situations and characters, as we have already had occasion to notice. This case is no exception. Belshazzar's first sentence to Daniel shows us that we have been deceived by the motif of the unknown hero. The king says "You are that Daniel, one of the exiles from Judah, whom the king my father brought from Judah" (vs. 13). The queen has not mentioned that Daniel is an exile from Judah. Belshazzar knows this already. He not only knows of Daniel and Daniel's background, but he describes Daniel with the stigma of his own obsession: "one of the exiles from Judah, whom *the king my father* brought from Judah." Moreover, he refuses to use the name given to Daniel by his father. (Is that name, Belteshazzar, too close to his own?)

Lacocque, then, is on target in that Belshazzar does know of Daniel and does indeed resist acknowledging him. On the other hand, Belshazzar never professes—as Lacocque would have it—"ignorance of Daniel's existence." Nor does Belshazzar fail to remember Daniel because of some sort of "mental block" or "psychological barrier" (Lacocque, 97). Belshazzar remembers Daniel quite well; he remembers well enough to know that he is an exile from Judah.

So, what is going on between the sovereign and the sage? The following reading suggests an answer.

Belshazzar has overtly shunned Daniel because Daniel is a symbol of his father's regime. First of all, Daniel the exile falls into the same category as do the temple vessels. They were both brought from Judah by Nebuchadnezzar, the king, the father. Daniel, like the vessels, symbolizes the success of Nebuchadnezzar, a success that Belshazzar would like to belittle. Moreover, Daniel was respected and admired by Nebuchadnezzar. He occupied an important place in Nebuchadnezzar's administration. What Belshazzar has attempted to show with the vessels, he has also attempted to show with Daniel: What was important to his father is not important to him.

We might also see an association between Daniel and the queen. Neither was invited to Belshazzar's banquet. The queen comes unbidden. Perhaps she has not been invited because she, too, is too closely identified with the rule of Nebuchadnezzar. The reader may recall the situation that Bathsheba describes to David in 1 Kings 1. Those who threaten Adonijah's power have not been invited to his banquet.

When Belshazzar speaks to Daniel, he ignores Daniel's former position even though the queen has just gone to great lengths to remind him of it (Plöger, 87). Rather than saying "You are that Belteshazzar, one of the sages, whom my father the king promoted to be chief of the magicians, enchanters, Chaldeans, and astrologers . . . ," he says instead "You are that Daniel, one of the exiles of Judah, whom my father the king brought from Judah." His word choices minimize Daniel's status.

The tone of the remainder of Belshazzar's speech is very difficult to determine. Since he disregards Daniel's former status in his opening address, we should not imagine that his tone is one of a "friendly welcome and proposal" (Heaton, 160; cf. Lacocque, 98). If, as has been argued above, Belshazzar has shunned Daniel up to this point because the sage is too closely associated with Belshazzar's father, then it seems logical that Belshazzar would not be very happy about Daniel's presence. The two are face to face, however, "before the thousand." The king keeps his composure. He is torn between wanting to understand the writing and yet not wanting his father's chief sage to be the successful interpreter.

This ambivalence is borne out by the fact that, while Belshazzar uses many of the queen's glowing descriptions of Daniel and even words that Nebuchadnezzar used in chapter 4, he never expresses such confidence himself. He speaks (5:14-15) of Daniel's having "the spirit of the gods," and of "light, insight and wisdom" having been found in him and of Daniel's ability "to interpret" and "to solve problems," but he never uses these words as direct statements of confidence in Daniel. In chapter 4 Nebuchadnezzar says to Daniel, ". . . *I know* that the spirit of the holy gods is in you . . ." (4:9 [6]). Belshazzar says, "*I have heard of you,* that the spirit of the gods is in you and light and insight and excellent wisdom have been found in you" (5:14). In chapter 4, having related his dream, Nebuchadnezzar says, "And you, Belteshazzar, disclose the interpretation, because all the sages of my kingdom are not able to make known to me the interpretation, but *you are able* for the spirit of the holy gods is in you" (4:18 [15]). Belshazzar also speaks of the failure of the sages, but notice that he does not contrast so starkly their failure with Daniel's ability:

> "Now, the sages and the enchanters were brought before me who were to read this writing . . . but they were not able to disclose the interpretation . . . . *I have heard about you, that you are able* to give interpretations and to solve problems. Now, *if you are able* to read the writing and to make known to me its interpretation, you will be

clothed in purple and the chain of gold will be upon your neck and you will rule as third in the kingdom." (5:15-16)

There is a pattern to Belshazzar's speech:

A You are that Daniel, one of the exiles from Judah whom the king my father brought from Judah.

  B *I have heard of you,* that the spirit of the gods is in you and light and insight and excellent wisdom have been found in you.

    C The sages . . . were not able to disclose the interpretation of the matter.

  B' *I have heard of you,* that you are able to give interpretations and to solve problems.

A' Now, if you are able . . . you will rule as third in the kingdom.

Belshazzar's speech moves from pointing out Daniel's humble status to dangling before him the possibility of a position at the other end of the spectrum. Encased in this frame are two statements concerning Daniel's ability. They are not declarations of confidence, however, but statements of hearsay, statements that challenge Daniel to prove whether or not the descriptions of his ability are indeed correct. In the center of the speech, Belshazzar describes the failure of the other sages. At this pivotal point, the accent falls on *inability*. It is up to Daniel to prove himself different from the other sages. If he fails in this, he loses not only his so-called reputation, but a chance at power and prestige.

One might read Belshazzar's speech as tinged with skepticism, perhaps even sarcasm, but at the very least, as a speech of challenge. It has its counterpart in the speech of Nebuchadnezzar to Shadrach, Meshach and Abednego in 3:14-15. In chapter 3, accusation brings the three men before the king. In chapter 5, recommendation brings Daniel before the king. In chapter 3 the king questions the truth of the accusation. In chapter 5, it would seem, the king is questioning the truth of the recommendation. In chapter 3 the king is forced, on account of his earlier ultimatum, to threaten Shadrach, Meshach, and Abednego with death for their failure to obey. In chapter 5 the king is forced, on account of his earlier promise, to offer Daniel a reward for his success. Just as Nebuchadnezzar is surely not anxious to learn that his top officials, whom he himself appointed, have disobeyed his command, so Belshazzar is not anxious to see his father's chief sage succeed (particularly if the writing is an ill-omen) where his own sages have failed.

On the other hand, Belshazzar is a man divided. He has just seen an apparition that has terrified him and the fact that the apparition has not yet been explained has increased his anxiety even more. Perhaps, as Lacocque suggests (101), Belshazzar does suspect that the writing is a negative pronouncement.[14] If this is the case, then we must suppose that Belshazzar reacts to ill tidings as do most people: He does not want to know the bad news—but not knowing is worse. He needs to find out what the writing says, but he does not want Daniel to be the one to tell him. He is desperate, he is vulnerable, and he resents having to depend upon Daniel, the man who most represents his father's power and success.

Daniel 's Perspective: Verse 17

If one reads Belshazzar's speech as a complex mixture of skepticism, challenge, desperation, and resentment rather than a "friendly welcome," a "kindly invitation," and an "expression of confidence," then the brusqueness of Daniel's reply makes more sense.[15] Daniel is not returning indictment for courteous greeting; he is not railing against Belshazzar as an answer to compliments and expressions of confidence. Daniel is meeting the challenge. He hears the skepticism. He hears the disregard for his former status. He sees Belshazzar dangling the bait of reward.

Daniel waves aside the reward with an air of disdain: "You can keep your gifts; give your rewards to another" (vs. 17). Porteous notices that this refusal is out of character for Daniel. Obviously, he has no aversion to accepting rewards in chapter two. The reward itself is not the problem. The problem for Daniel is the person offering the reward. Daniel's refusal is designed to offend. His refusal is motivated not by his humility (Anderson, 59), but by his pride.

When E. W. Heaton (160) marvels that Daniel's "attitude is in striking contrast . . . with his generous concern for Nebuchadnezzar previously," he hits upon the key to Daniel's response. Let us look more closely at this contrast.

That Daniel is indeed "generously concerned" for Nebuchadnezzar is a point we noted when discussing chapter 4. Called upon to interpret the dream that he knows to be judgmental, he responds with tactful hesitancy. He does not want to explain to the king the dream's message and, when pressed by the king to do so, wishes aloud that the dream and its meaning would not befall the king. His opening sentence employs parallel clauses: "My lord, may the dream be for those who hate you and its interpretation be for your enemies!" (4:19 [16]). When Daniel responds to Belshazzar in chapter 5, he again uses parallel clauses, but this time without tact or protocol: "Your gifts can remain yours; give your rewards to another" (5:17). He offensively refuses the king's reward but hurriedly volunteers to read and interpret the writing, writing that he knows to predict Belshazzar's downfall. He never hesitates, but enters into his task of indictment with unsurpassed zeal.

Daniel's Interpretation: Verses 18-29

After agreeing to read and interpret the writing, he begins as he has begun many times before: "You, O King . . ." (Cf. 2:29, 31, 37, 38; 4:22 [19]). From our experience with this phrase, we expect him to start talking about the king's vision (2:29, 31) or about how the king's vision relates to his power (2:37, 38; 4:22 [19]). Since all of the dreams and visions thus far have been concerned with royal power, we might expect something like 2:37: "You, O King, to whom the God of heaven gave the kingdom, the power, the might and the glory . . . ." And indeed, Daniel's address starts this way: "You, O King, the most high god gave the kingdom and the greatness and the glory and the majesty to—Nebuchadnezzar your father" (5:18). With these words, Daniel stings Belshazzar in his most sensitive spot. What the young king has desired most—power, prestige, authority—has not been attributed to him, but to the man whose memory he has tried to defeat—his father.

On Nebuchadnezzar, the Father

In all of Daniel's dealings with Nebuchadnezzar, the issue has been the recognition of the divine source of royal power. By recapitulating the god-given power of Nebuchadnezzar and his experience of humiliation when he grew presumptuous, Daniel is communicating several things. First, he is reminding Belshazzar and the audience that Nebuchadnezzar's problem was, indeed, bound up with acknowledging the most high god as the source of his power. Second, he is taunting Belshazzar with the extent of his father's power: ". . . all the peoples, nations, and languages came to tremble and fear before him. He killed whomever he pleased and he kept alive whomever he pleased; he raised up whomever he pleased and he put down whomever he pleased . . ." (vs. 19). Daniel's language is surprising (cf. Lacocque, 101). He is describing the power of Nebuchadnezzar with language normally only used to describe the power of God (cf. Deut 32:39; 1 Sam 2:7; Ps 75:8; Job 5:11-16). With these words, Daniel flaunts the power of the former king before the son who desires to surpass it. Of course, Daniel makes a point of mentioning that the most high god gave this divine-like power to Nebuchadnezzar—which is the final point of his recitation concerning that king. Daniel's implication is that God has given no such power to Belshazzar. Belshazzar has tried to grasp what will never be his.

Because the power given to Nebuchadnezzar was so great, implies Daniel, the overextension of his pride was inevitable. Daniel speaks as though, given such power, it was only a matter of *when* his heart would be lifted up in pride (vs. 20). In a sense, then, Daniel excuses Nebuchadnezzar for the fact that, eventually, his spirit was hardened. As in chapter 4, Daniel refrains from passing personal judgment on him.

Daniel has continued on about Nebuchadnezzar for four long verses and has yet to come to the problem of the writing on the wall. His role thus far has not been that of a sage but of an indicting prophet (cf. Collins, 68). This portrayal has been compared to the depictions of Amos, Jeremiah before Zedekiah, and Nathan before David (cf. Anderson, 59; Towner 1984:74; Lacocque, 101). There is, however, an important difference between this speech of Daniel and those of those prophets. Daniel makes no effort to clarify his speech as the "word of the Lord." Daniel speaks on his own cognizance. His praise and memory of Nebuchadnezzar is reflective of the "generous concern" and admiration that Daniel has expressed to Nebuchadnezzar in both chapters 2 and 4.

On Belshazzar, the Son

As he moves from citing the occurrences of the past to accusing Belshazzar directly, his tone changes. He has no problems of conscience as he has when required to relay the message of judgment to Nebuchadnezzar in chapter 4. He makes no effort to soften the tidings or to disengage himself from the indictment; he is in complete agreement with his message. How curious that Daniel's attitude toward the king corresponds directly to his position and esteem (or, in this case, lack of position and esteem). When he is the king's chief sage, his message is one of discretion, even when it means underreading the judgment of God. When his position is ignored, when he is ostracized from the administration, Daniel's word is a harsh word, delivered without tact, without respect. Daniel's objectivity is questionable.

His indictment reveals that he, too, knows many things that he has not been told. Belshazzar has not told him any of the events that have led up to the writing. He has not mentioned the vessels, the drinking, or the worship of idols. He has not even told Daniel about the hand. Daniel, upon entering the banquet hall, has obviously assessed the situation for himself. Since Belshazzar does not put the writing in context, Daniel does. The writing has to do with Belshazzar's behavior.

Notice that, in his indictment of Belshazzar, Daniel does not single out the desecration of the vessels as the reason for judgment. None of the accusations are subordinated; they are all connected by "and." All stand on equal ground:

> "You . . . have not lowered your heart . . . and you have lifted yourself to the lord of heaven . . . and the vessels from his house have been brought . . . and you and your lords, your wives and your concubines have drunk wine from them and you have praised the gods of silver and gold, bronze, iron, wood, and stone . . . and you have not glorified the God who holds your breath in his hand and whose are all your ways." (5:22-23)

Daniel has an investment in the very content of his message as well. Belshazzar has not respected the king who commanded Daniel's strong allegiance. Belshazzar has desecrated the vessels sacred to Daniel and his people. And finally, Belshazzar has ignored Daniel's God. Like the lord of heaven, Daniel takes offense at Belshazzar's behavior.

Daniel's speech not only tells us something about Daniel's own character, but in his indictment of Belshazzar we glimpse also how he views this king's character. According to Daniel, Belshazzar's character, and consequently his punishable behavior, must be understood in light of the character of his father. The emphatic "You" loosely parallels and contrasts the indictment with the part of the speech that recounts Nebuchadnezzar's glory and subsequent pride and humiliation.

You, O King, the most high God gave the kingdom, the greatness, the glory, and majesty to Nebuchadnezzar your father. On account of the greatness that he gave him, all peoples, nations and languages trembled and feared before him. He killed whomever he pleased and he kept alive whomever he pleased. He lifted up whomever he pleased and he put down whomever he pleased. And when his heart was lifted up and his spirit grew strong to make him presumptuous, he was brought down from the throne of his kingdom and his glory was taken from him. He was driven from the human community and his heart became like that of a beast and his dwelling was with the wild asses. He was fed grass as oxen are and his body wet from the dew of heaven, until he knew that the most high God rules in the human kingdom and he sets over it whomever he pleases. (5:18-21)

You, his son, Belshazzar, have not lowered your heart though you knew all of this. You have lifted yourself to the lord of heaven and the vessels of his house have been brought before you and your lords, your wives and concubines have drunk wine from them and you have praised the gods of silver and gold, bronze, iron, wood and stone who do not see and who do not hear and who do not know. And the God who has your breath in his hand and whose are all your ways, you have not glorified. Then from before him the palm of the hand has been sent and this writing has been inscribed. And this is the writing which is inscribed: Mene, mene, tekel, and parsin. This is the interpretation of the word: Mene—God has numbered the days of your kingdom and has finished it. Tekel—you have been weighed on the balances and have been found wanting. Peres—your kingdom has been broken in two and given to Media and Persia. (5:22-28)

Several opposing images recur in this roughly paralleled speech: lifting and lowering, life and death, power and impotence, taking and giving. These opposing images reinforce Daniel's message that Belshazzar the son stands in direct contrast to Nebuchadnezzar the father. Nebuchadnezzar, suggests Daniel, had lifted his heart understandably: God had given him divine-like power,[16] power over life and death itself. In contrast, Belshazzar his son has lifted himself without reason; he does not truly comprehend life and death, much less have power over them. His ignorance and his subsequent impotence is evidenced, from Daniel's point of view, by his trust in idols. The gods he considers to be alive "do not see, do not hear, and do not know." Conversely, the God who is the source and controller of life he does not even recognize.

Nebuchadnezzar had to be brought low, Daniel intimates, in order to learn that the power he enjoyed was a gift from a sovereign higher than he. But rather than learning a lesson and lowering his own heart, Belshazzar has tried to lift himself higher than his father by attempting to *take* what was *given* to his father as a *gift.* This action is symbolized by his taking and using the captured vessels. The power was a gift to his father. The vessels were a gift to his father. In his attempt to surpass his father, he has collided with the only sovereign more powerful than his father—the lord of heaven. In his attempt to seize the gifts, he has offended the giver.

The power of Nebuchadnezzar set him apart from his subjects: "All peoples, nations, and languages trembled before him" (vs. 19). Belshazzar, on the other hand, is pictured consorting with his entourage, engaging in the same offensive behavior—behavior for which he is responsible: "You and your lords, your wives and your concubines have drunk wine from [the vessels]" (vs. 23). Before the father's power all peoples trembled. When the son asserts his power the courtiers carouse. In his concern to glorify himself, he has had no regard even for those around him let alone his people at large. He has led his lords and ladies to treat as common what is holy and to treat as holy what is in fact common (gold, silver, bronze, iron, wood, stone)—though notice that Daniel directs the latter accusation, appropriately, at the king alone: "and *you* have praised the gods of silver and gold . . ." (vs. 23; cf. vs. 4).

In short, Daniel sees Belshazzar as an audacious but weak king. Indeed, it would appear that to Daniel, he *is* audacious *because* he is weak. (In other words, some presumption is excusable if one is truly strong like Nebuchadnezzar.) Daniel's characterization of Belshazzar is supported by the narrator's portrayal. Belshazzar's problem with his father is itself a sign of the young king's insecurity. He cannot conceal his fear; he fails to command with authority (he "cries aloud"); he promises excessive reward (where his father might have threatened punishment; cf. chapter 2); he allows the queen mother to take control. All could be construed as evidences of weakness on the part of an absolute monarch.

A Question of Value

The contrast between Belshazzar and his father opens up an interpretation of the writing on the wall (vss. 24-28).[17] The actual words of the writing, Mene, mene, tekel, and parsin, are ambiguous in that they not only represent weights of coinage, but also play upon the verbs "to count or number," "to weigh," and "to divide" as can be seen in Daniel's interpretation. Furthermore, *parsin* or *peres* (as Daniel has it) plays upon *paras,* "Persian."[18] The image of coinage and the verbs themselves (that is, the words on the wall and Daniel's interpretation of them) both suggest that the issue is one of *value.* And, indeed, the problem of value has been the crux of the story. Belshazzar has not valued his father's example. He has not valued the captured vessels. He has not valued his father's chief sage. He has not valued his father's God. Instead, he has valued the services of incapable sages. He has valued gods who do not see, who do not hear, and who do not know.

The portrayal of Belshazzar as a weak king communicates also the irony that the man of inappropriate values is himself of little value. He is of little value to Daniel; he is of little value to God. Thus the images of weights and balances fit comfortably with the images of lifting and lowering: the weak king of little value has tried to lift himself, that is, make himself valuable, but to no avail. "You have been weighed in the balances and have been found wanting," says Daniel (vs. 27). Weighed against whom? According to this reading—Nebuchadnezzar. If Nebuchadnezzar is a minah, Belshazzar is only a shekel (a ratio of 60 to 1) and while the Medes and Persians (half-minahs) may be less valuable than Nebuchadnezzar, they are a good deal better than Belshazzar.

Value answers the question that centuries of readers have posed to this story: Why, when the notorious Nebuchadnezzar is given a chance to repent, is Belshazzar not also allowed repentance? Surely, after seeing the dislocated handwriting on the wall, he would be an easy convert! The common answer that the violation of holy things is unforgivable is not entirely satisfactory.[19] If it were simply the act of desecration itself at issue, like the desecration of Israel's ancient ark of the covenant (cf. 1 Sam 6:19, 2 Sam 6:6-7), then all the people participating would be liable. All would be condemned. Instead, Belshazzar alone is condemned.

Belshazzar's sin is not so much a ritual sin as it is a sin of presumption. It is not clear, however, as Lacocque (95) reads the text, that Belshazzar intends to challenge God directly when he uses the vessels:

> Through his profanatory act, the king has 'desired' the writing on the wall. He has challenged God and his challenge has been accepted. It is solely an affair between God and Belshazzar . . . .

The problem with seeing Belshazzar's act as a direct challenge to God is that, in order to challenge someone, one must at least implicitly acknowledge the existence of the person one is challenging. Part of Belshazzar's transgression is that he has not acknowledged, he has not glorified the God who gives and controls life.

Furthermore, though his act is obviously offensive to the lord of heaven, his transgression is not an issue strictly confined to Belshazzar and God. Nebuchadnezzar haunts this exchange: he is the standard that Belshazzar has tried to surpass; he is the standard by whom Belshazzar is to be judged. Their sins are the same. Nebuchadnezzar, however, was valuable enough to God to have been spared in spite of his presumption. His redeeming quality was his strength. Strong kings can be successful agents.

At issue here is the matter of sovereignty. The conversion of Nebuchadnezzar, a great king, is a notable stroke for the sovereignty of God. Belshazzar, on the other hand, is a weak king and, because he is weak, his presumption is magnified. He is of no use to God. He is "found wanting" and though, after seeing the vision, he might be an easy convert, he is not worthy of divine investment. His kingdom is to be finished, his account to be settled. The gift of the kingdom is to be taken away and given to someone else, because after all, "the Most High God rules in the human kingdom and sets over it whomever he pleases" (vs. 21).

Daniel's Control

It is not only Nebuchadnezzar who casts his shadow over this "affair between God and Belshazzar." So also does Daniel. From the minute he opens his mouth to speak, Daniel demands our attention and thereby controls the story. The question arises, What is the extent of his control, both over the story world and over our reading of the story world? In determining an answer, we might explore another question: Given the events of the earlier stories, what might we expect to happen?

In chapters 2, 3, and 4, the divine message or theophany is designed to evoke the king's response. In these stories, God speaks a word of judgment, God communicates in order to bring about a change in understanding, in order to redeem, if you will. In Daniel 5, however, Belshazzar is given no final word; we are not allowed to see his reaction. Instead, Daniel fills the stage. Daniel cuts off the possibility of response in two ways: First, if there *is* a way that Belshazzar can avoid or escape punishment (as there is in 4:27 [24]), Daniel does not tell him of it. Second, Daniel opens no ears to confession.

Consequently, the role of Daniel and the role of God become blurred just as do the words of Daniel and the words of God. Daniel himself certainly never bothers to distinguish between his words and those of God. What motivates Daniel's indictment of Belshazzar? All of this speech cannot be derived from merely four words written on a wall. Daniel's complaint is the same as that of the lord of heaven. Belshazzar has ignored both of them. He has failed to glorify Daniel and he has failed to glorify Daniel's God. (We might compare the complaint of Samuel in 1 Samuel 8.) Instead, he has trusted in gods incapable of doing what Daniel's God can do, just as he has trusted in sages who are incapable of doing what Daniel can do. Does Daniel's arrogance mirror God's impatience with the weak and stupid king? Or is Daniel's resentment being projected upon God? Daniel and God are so closely aligned, how can one clearly separate between them?

We must rely on Daniel not just to interpret the words on the wall, but also to tell us what the words are. He does not pray for revelation as he does in chapter two; he already knows what the writing says. He does not feel the need to attribute his ability to God. Everyone knows that he has the spirit of the holy gods in him. He does not even bother to clarify that the spirit is of but one holy god. Daniel may as well be the hand that writes upon the wall; they function the same way, as the word play, "to loosen knots" suggests: The anxiety incurred by the vision of the hand is anxiety verified in Daniel's solving of the problem of the writing. Daniel's word confirms that the word on the wall is a word of death. If Belshazzar's "knots are loosened" at the appearance of the hand, surely Daniel's words have loosened them further.

How ironic that Daniel grows ever more like his friend Nebuchadnezzar. He wields the words of life and death as easily as this king wields power over life and death (5:19). Moreover, it appears at least from chapters 4 and 5, that Daniel, like Nebuchadnezzar, "lifts up whomever he pleases" and "puts down whomever he pleases." In both cases, authority is God-given, but both have trouble making the source of their authority clear.

Daniel does not simply read and interpret for us the writing on the wall. He interprets for us the story itself. Just as he puts the writing on the wall in the context of the drinking feast, he puts the character Belshazzar in the context of his past. He confirms our suspicion that the character of Belshazzar is to be read in light of the character of Nebuchadnezzar. He suggests to us that as he finds Nebuchadnezzar's sin excusable but not Belshazzar's, so should we.[20]

When Daniel's speech is finished, Belshazzar confers upon him the promised reward (vs. 29). As many commentators have noticed, it is rather odd that Daniel now accepts what previously he had refused.[21] If Daniel's initial refusal of reward is read as an act of humility or an example of "what the attitude of Jewish sage to a heathen potentate ought to be" (Porteous, 81), then his later acceptance has to be suppressed. In fact, any discussion of Daniel that interprets his character to be flawless (for example, Anderson, 59, 62) must ignore or qualify this part of the story. But if we take the difference in his behavior to be significant, it is not difficult to account for it. As has been observed, Daniel accepts the reward now, when Belshazzar, after hearing the stinging, condemning message of doom, cannot possibly be happy to give it (Hartman and DiLella, 190). Perhaps that is the very reason why he accepts it. Allowing Belshazzar to do what he obviously does not want to do is Daniel's final retaliation—and assertion of control. Perhaps, then, he takes the honor and position now as a symbol of victory over Belshazzar. Belshazzar has previously ignored his position as chief sage; Daniel now overcomes the king's attempt to ostracize him. Perhaps he accepts the honor and position now because he, too, values power and prestige.

Belshazzar the Chaldean and Darius the Mede: Verses 30-31 [5:30-6:1]

The story ends almost as abruptly as it begins: "That night Belshazzar, the Chaldean king, was killed. And Darius the Mede took the kingdom. He was sixty-two years old" (vss. 30-31 [5:30-6:1]). The narrator connects these two events only chronologically; the audience must make any causal connections. We are not told who kills Belshazzar or how, but simply that he is killed. We are not told how Darius takes the kingdom, simply that he does. The information continues the ironic thread of the story. First, the young king, so anxious to prove himself, is defeated by an old king. Second, the word *qabel*, "to take," also means "to receive"; hence we are given alternative ways to read the coda, a choice which sustains the ambiguity of the king's perception. In Darius's point of view, is the kingdom a conquest or is it a gift? And what of *our* point of view as readers? What perspective are we being led to adopt? Does Darius take the kingdom or does he receive it from another hand? And if from another hand, whose? The hand of the lord of heaven or the hand of the third ruler in the kingdom?

The Human and the Divine

No matter how negatively Daniel interprets the character of Belshazzar, the story's ending is somewhat unsettling. Perhaps this is because the oppositions in the story are not so clear. Divine sovereignty and human sovereignty do not stand opposed to one another as one might expect. Instead, they are in a hierarchical relationship: Divine sovereignty takes priority over human sovereignty. At the same time, however, the hierarchy is twisted in that the two cannot always be distinguished, as we have seen in the descriptions of Nebuchadnezzar's power and Daniel's ability, and as we have heard in the ambiguously motivated words of Daniel himself.

Furthermore, the two entities, the divine and the human, are inconsistent within themselves. We may be led to think that, in the realm of humanity, there also exists an opposition between humility and pride, as is imaged so well in the lifting and lowering language of Daniel's speech. God desires both humility and pride. On the one hand, the human sovereign is to be humble in relation to God. On the other hand, God respects, desires the human sovereign to be proud and powerful in relation to other humans. But here, too, the two elements are not strictly opposed to one another; they relate hierarchically. According to chapters 4 and 5, (religious) humility is a more desirable quality to God than is pride. Divine sovereignty and its counterpart, human humility, may be the priorities of the narrative, but the hierarchy keeps breaking down. What cracks the hierarchy is the fact that (humble) humans—the characters, the narrator, the audience—must confer sovereignty on the divine in order for divine sovereignty to emerge as the point of the story. In other words, the fact that divine sovereignty is dependent upon human acknowledgment undercuts the idea that God authorizes and controls human sovereignty (cf. Gunn's reading of the exodus story, 1982:89).

Another twisted relationship between the human and the divine in the stories of chapters 4 and 5 has to do with revelation and interpretation. Divine knowledge and wisdom take priority over human knowledge and wisdom. However, while Daniel's ability is dependent upon God's revelation, God is dependent upon Daniel's ability to interpret in order that divine revelation can be made known. Moreover, the problem of perspective (or point of view) further muddles the hierarchy. If the other characters do not clearly distinguish between Daniel's wisdom and divine wisdom, then how can they perceive that God's wisdom is indeed sovereign?

(Divine) revelation and (human) interpretation present yet another unsettling irony. Daniel (as God's representative) dramatizes the tenuous connections among sovereignty, revelation, and the issue of life and death. The God who speaks judgment in chapter 4 speaks to redeem. The divine word of judgment brings a new understanding, a new knowledge of God. In Nebuchadnezzar's case, the new knowledge feeds back into God's sovereignty. The greatness of the spokesperson contributes to the greatness of God. However, the God who speaks judgment in chapter 5 speaks to kill. A testimony from Belshazzar would add nothing to the sovereignty of God. Consequently, pride and humility fall into a double bind: One must be proud in order for one's humility to be valued by God! And Daniel, in his wisdom, in his godlike knowledge, issues reprieve in one instance and a sentence of death in the other (and, we might add, in the latter case, without a word of humility). It is at the end of chapter 5 that we realize that there is contradiction in the nature of God and, likewise, in the nature of human beings.

We began our discussion of chapter 5 by noticing that it was significantly related to chapter 3. The analogies we have found between these stories have helped us to answer some questions that we have asked of chapter 5. There are other analogies between the two chapters that have not been discussed, broader analogies that perhaps raise more questions than they answer. We pointed out earlier that, in each story, the worship of images plays a strategic role. Shadrach, Meshach and Abednego are condemned because they do not worship the image of gold. The three Judean exiles do not worship the king's god. In chapter 5 there is an ironic reversal. Belshazzar is condemned because he does worship images and because he does not worship the exiles' god. In chapter 3 the king asks the three men before him, "Who is the god who will deliver you from my hands?" In chapter 5, there are also hands at work, not the hands of the king, but the hands of God: One hand holds breath and life; the other silently writes words of death. In chapter 3 the king passes a death sentence upon the exiles; in chapter 5, an exile passes a death sentence upon the king. In chapter 3, the exiles are allowed to defend themselves; in chapter 5, the king is not. In chapter 3 the exiles are saved from religious persecution; in chapter 5, the king is not.

As these broader comparisons and contrasts indicate, there are little needles in this theme of sovereignty. The issue of power touches not only the kings, but the exiles as well. The powerless exiles grow progressively more powerful with each story. The God of the conquered proves with each episode, as in the repeated hardenings of Pharaoh's heart, to be the victor. And the victorious God's representatives grow more and more self-secure—self-secure in their judgment, self-secure in their indictment, self-secure in their interpretation. In short, the powerful are entrusted with making divine revelation known.[22] But, we might ask, can the powerful be trusted?

Chapter Six

DANIEL 6

ALL THE KING'S MEN

Darius's Government:
Verses 1-6 [2-7]

Darius, busy setting up his new regime, decides to decentralize the government. He appoints 120 provincial officials and three prime ministers to whom the officials answer. Daniel is one of the three. He distinguishes himself above the other two ministers (which comes as no surprise to the reader) and Darius intends to set him over the kingdom. The jealousy of the other officials provides the story's conflict. When they cannot find any fault in Daniel about which they can tattle to the king, the officials scheme to entrap Daniel in his piety.

This exposition provokes reminiscence as well as anticipation. "Darius the Mede took (or received) the kingdom" both ends the story of Belshazzar (and so is 5:31 in English versions) and begins the story of Darius (and so is 6:1 in the Masoretic Text). The sentence forges a union between the stories from the beginning. Young king and old king, rejected sage and distinguished sage, a kingdom's end and a kingdom's beginning, all stand linked through this transition. Having read animosity between Belshazzar and Daniel in chapter 5, we might now see Daniel's political progress in chapter 6 as a sign of his final ascendancy over the young king. Daniel, ostracized from the administration like Nebuchadnezzar before him, returns with even greater power and prestige—whereas Belshazzar who had tried to exclude him from power has passed into oblivion.

Darius's appointment of three prime ministers plays upon Belshazzar's begrudging promotion of Daniel to "third ruler in the kingdom," giving the impression that Darius is simply adopting the existent political structure of the newly acquired kingdom. Daniel does not have to be introduced to Darius; he is already part of the power structure. In fact, Darius is so well disposed toward Daniel that one might suspect that Daniel, as third ruler in the kingdom, has welcomed with open arms Darius's takeover. The narrator, after all, tells us that Daniel "distinguished himself . . . because of the excellent spirit in him" (vs. 3 [4]). Daniel's "excellent spirit" has previously referred to his ability to interpret mysteries. As far as we know, however, he has not been called upon to interpret anything for Darius; rather, in the context of chapter 6, the excellent spirit appears to refer to political ability. Of course, the last time we saw Daniel's excellent spirit at work (5:12, 14ff.), he was not only interpreting mysteries but also undermining Belshazzar's rule. Perhaps it was that particular manifestation of excellent spirit that brought him his present distinction.

In a sense, the rule of Darius represents a return to the latter days of Nebuchadnezzar as portrayed in chapter 4. The phrase "it seemed good" begins both stories. In chapter 4, "it seems good" to Nebuchadnezzar to render authority to the Most High. In chapter 6, "it seems good" to Darius to render authority to other people, in particular, to Daniel. The suggestion of a parallel may prompt us to observe a more substantial similarity. Both stories depict the relationship between sage and sovereign to be one of amiability and cooperation, unlike the stories found in chapters 3 and 5 in which the relationship between sage and sovereign is not without friction and opposition. Both Nebuchadnezzar of chapter 4 and Darius of chapter 6 have the utmost respect for Daniel's ability. Of course, by chapter 6, Daniel's ability has advanced from personal interpretive and counseling skills (chapter 4) to political expertise.

Daniel's ability and his king's admiration give rise to obvious jealousy on the part of the other ministers and officials. Although they try to catch Daniel in a subversive act, they are unsuccessful because, as the narrator tells us, Daniel is "faithful and neither neglect nor fault could be found regarding him" (vs. 4 [5]). They know, however, that Daniel has a certain religious allegiance and, while this does not normally conflict with his political allegiance, the officials scheme to set these allegiances on a collision course (vs. 5 [6]).

The Prohibition: Verses 6-9 [7-10]

The next episode finds the ministers and officials coming before the king to put their plan into action: "Then these prime ministers and provincial officials made a commotion (*rgš*) before the king and thus they said to him . . ." (vs. 6 [7]).[1] Their reason for coming before the king is clear to the reader; the narrator has already indicated what is about to transpire. Their reason, however, is not clear to the king. The pairing of *rgš* (which I am translating "to make a commotion") with the multipurpose preposition *ʿal* ("to," "over," "against," etc.) reflects what is, from the king's point of view, an ambiguous reason for the assembly. The ministers and officials are making a commotion *to* (or before) the king which, obviously, he perceives since they have come to him with their suggestion. The king might also interpret the men to be making a commotion *over* him since their request has to do with his own exaltation. What the king most likely does not consider, however, is the possibility that the men are making a commotion *against* him.

The officials come, addressing the king with the appropriate etiquette ("O King, live forever!"), and inform him:

> "All the prime ministers of the kingdom, the prefects, the provincial officials, the counselors and the governors have agreed that the king is to establish an ordinance and to authorize a prohibition that anyone who petitions any god or human being for thirty days, other than you, O King, will be cast into a den of lions. Now, O King, you must establish the prohibition and sign the document so that it does not change according to the law of the Medes and Persians which does not pass away [or, cannot be revoked]." (6:6-8 [7-9])

The men are lying, of course, about who has been involved in this agreement. Obviously Daniel has not consented. The story's exposition makes clear, moreover, that only the two other prime ministers and the provincial officials have discussed the matter: The prefects, the counselors and the governors have not been consulted. The lie is a tactic of persuasion. The men lead the king to believe that this opinion poll is exhaustive and unanimous.

The content of the speech belies its intent. We know that the goal of the recommendation is the entrapment and destruction of Daniel. Nothing on the surface betrays this intention, however. The speech appears to be a political proposal aimed at getting the king to confirm publicly his personal authority—a pretext that is brilliantly plausible given the newly established kingdom and Darius's plans for governing it. Darius has decentralized the government, an action which may be more efficient in the long run, but which also diminishes his own power. The officials' proposition implies that there may be a hidden danger in the king's plan: A powerful appointee might easily sway the people's allegiance away from the new king. The proposal, therefore, looks as though it is designed to rectify any threats to royal power that might be inherent in the king's political strategy. Thus, the vehicle of conspiracy is presented, ironically, as a protection *against* conspiracy!

This overture to the king has a delicately balanced appeal. The officials have weighed carefully Darius's propensity toward the redistribution of power. They are aware that he is not a rigid authoritarian at heart. Consequently, when they propose that he alone be the focus of his subjects' petitions, they suggest it as a temporary condition only. After all, the kingdom is new and, to some extent, unstable. The king should firmly establish his hold at the very beginning, they imply; then, when the new government is stable, the king can relax his grip.

Thus, despite the fact that it runs counter to his political policy but desiring, like any king, to make his kingdom sound, Darius is willing to accept the measure.

He appears to be oblivious to the absurdity implicit in this "temporary" measure. How can an ordinance in effect only thirty days be an edict that "cannot change"? How can a human being replace the divine—and for only thirty days at that, as if one could put on and take off divinity as one would a suit of clothes?[2]

The situation abounds with irony. The dramatic irony—the disparity between what the characters know and what we, the readers, know—allows us to recognize the verbal irony—the use of words to express something other than what they seem on the surface to mean. Because we know more than Darius does, we are able to recognize what he does not, namely, that the proposal is a ruse. While the prohibition seems to be protecting the king's interests, it is in fact subverting them. While the officials seem to be concentrating all power in king's hands, the king, by signing the edict, is actually falling into the power of the officials. Darius perceives that the men are making a commotion *over* him, but in fact they are making a commotion *against* him. He thinks that he is the focus of their proposal, but in fact the focus of their proposal is Daniel. When he signs the edict without discussion, he understands himself to be doing a sensible thing; we know, however, that he is doing a foolish thing that will surely come back to haunt him.

The Confrontation: Verses 10-13 [11-14]

Learning of the new edict, Daniel goes deliberately to his house to say his daily prayers (vs. 10). The narrator tells us that Daniel customarily prays three times a day in an upper chamber before an open window facing Jerusalem. Because his practice is observable and on a consistent schedule, the other ministers and officials have no difficulty catching him in the act, making petition to his god (vs. 11).

The men waste no time bringing the matter to the king's attention (vs. 12). Like the "certain Chaldeans" in chapter 3, they come with an accusation. However, unlike the Chaldeans who state the situation forthright ("You, O king, made a decree . . ." [3:10]), the officials in chapter 6 begin by addressing a question to the king: "O king, did you not sign an edict that anyone who makes a petition to any god or human being for thirty days—except to you, O King—would be cast into a den of lions?" The king replies: "The word is true according to the law of the Medes and the Persians which will never pass away" (vs. 12).

The form of this interchange reflects the way these men have carried out their conspiracy. By persuading the king to sign the edict in the first place, they have tricked him into unknowingly participating in the conspiracy against his favorite administrator. It is the king's edict that ensnares Daniel. Likewise, the question that the officials direct to the king lures the king into confirming the accusation against Daniel. The king's answer seals Daniel's fate.

Once the king has committed himself, the officials spring the trap: "That Daniel, who is one of the exiles from Judah, shows no deference to you, O king, or to the edict that you signed. Three times a day he makes his petition" (vs. 13). They make this formal accusation against Daniel with words that disparage and malign. He is not Daniel the prime minister, but Daniel the exile. He does not simply disregard the edict; he shows no deference to the king whatsoever. The men have equated the edict with some sort of oath of loyalty. Disobedience makes Daniel a complete traitor to the king. Besides, the fact that he is an exile makes him all the more suspect: Prisoners of war would be more inclined to subversion.

Although the accusation may be a gross overstatement, the reader also knows that there is some truth to it: Daniel does petition his god three times a day. Perhaps Darius, too, is aware of Daniel's piety—Is this is why he seeks no clarification of the nature of Daniel's daily petition? This episode raises questions about the preceding one. If Darius is conscious of Daniel's religiosity (as are the officials), how can he believe the men when they tell him (in vs. 7 [8]) that *all* the prime ministers agree on the edict? If he knows about Daniel, has he temporarily forgotten? Is he so swept along by the crowd that he does not consider the ramifications of this decree? Does he think that Daniel is willing to make an exception for thirty days? Why does he not notice that Daniel is not among the men before him?

If Darius knows, or at least remembers, Daniel's piety when the men make their accusation, then perhaps this explains why Darius, unlike Nebuchadnezzar in chapter 3, does not call the accused before him for a hearing. If Daniel's worship habits are known, there is no reason to allow him to defend himself. Such a reading does not explain, however, why Darius fails even to question the unqualified charge that "he shows no deference to you." Does this part of the indictment not sink in? Possibly—but perhaps this indictment, too, is credible from Darius's perspective. Consider Daniel's relationship to the last king. Daniel certainly "showed no deference" to Belshazzar. Could there be, in Darius's mind, the slightest suspicion of Daniel's political allegiance, a little, gnawing suspicion that contributes to his "displeasure" upon hearing the accusation? Darius wrestles with himself concerning Daniel. But he grants Daniel no hearing.

The King's Dilemma: Verses 14-18 [15-19]

Darius, says the narrator, "set his heart upon Daniel to deliver him and until the setting of the sun, he was struggling to rescue him" (vs. 14 [15]). What the king's options are, we are not told at this point. We are not sure of the nature of the king's struggle. He must have been aware of some alternative course of action, however, because in the next scene the officials feel the need to coerce the king to see the sentence through (vs. 15 [16]).

The men again make a commotion, and the king is surely aware by this time that they are making a commotion, not innocently *to* him and certainly not *over* him, but indeed *against* him. The men drop all protocol; they make no effort to be polite. They speak with an imperative: "Know, O King, that it is a law of the Medes and Persians that any edict or ordinance that the king establishes is not to change" (vs. 15 [16]). Is it indeed the case that the law *cannot* be changed? Why must the men remind him and in such an unpleasant tone? Is it not the case that their imperative carries with it a veiled threat, an implicit ultimatum? What is the law? It is the opposite of anarchy. The law that does not change represents stability. If the king changes the law—and doubtless loopholes exist or the king would have nothing to wrestle over—then the kingdom will be weakened. The king's power is questionable. Are the men not telling Darius that, if he changes the law, they will bring his power into question in a very tangible way? They are many; they are organized (the fact that they are portrayed as a collective character reinforces their unity); and, despite the fact that they are *supposed* to be "throughout the kingdom," they are all present in the capital city ready to make a political move, if need be.

Darius cannot afford to endanger his kingdom (or his kingship) even for the sake of a favorite, particularly if the loyalty of that favorite is in doubt. So he commands that Daniel be brought and thrown into the lions' den (vs. 16 [17]).

At this point he offers a wistful kind of petition of his own. To Daniel (probably out of earshot in the pit), the king says: "May your god, whom you serve continually, deliver you." We might hear in these words a mixture of respect, displeasure, and pathos. The king's admires Daniel for his courage in serving his god despite the edict. That much is clear. He seems to think that Daniel's courage deserves just reward from his god. But whether or not Darius is truly convinced that Daniel's god will save him is another matter. More likely he fears that Daniel's god will be of no avail; he laments that Daniel's allegiance has brought him to such an end. Might he not realize, sadly and perhaps a little bitterly, that if Daniel had served his king (rather than his god) continually, his king could have and would have gladly delivered him?

A stone is put over the mouth of the den and, with a gesture of finality, Darius seals the stone with his signet and with the signet of his lords (vs. 17 [18]). The use of the royal signets symbolizes that Daniel's fate is sealed for the sake of the kingdom's stability.

If Daniel's night with the lions is, implicitly, wakeful, Darius's night in his palace is, explicitly, sleepless and stressful (vs. 18 [19]). Just as in chapter 3 we were not allowed to see inside the furnace, so, too, here we are not allowed inside the pit. We must spend the night with Darius and, for the first time in the story, we know no more than Darius does. Darius spends the night fasting and without diversions. Whether or not his fasting has religious significance is debatable. More likely he has trouble stomaching food knowing that this very night his favorite Daniel *is*, himself, food for the lions.

Deliverance: Verses 19-25 [20-26]

When the day breaks, the king returns to the den (vs. 19 [20]), perhaps on the chance that Daniel has survived the night, perhaps so that he can claim any of Daniel's remains for burial. Darius is still troubled and he cries out (*z'q*) in an anguished voice:

> "Daniel, servant of the living God, has your god, whom you serve continually, been able to deliver you?" (6:20 [21])

That he addresses Daniel does not imply that he has confidence in Daniel's survival. This is a cry of distress—*z'q* usually means to cry for help or in distress, not simply to call out (loudly). As David, in 2 Sam 18:33 [19:1], cries out (*z'q*) to the dead Absalom, the Absalom who was guilty of treason, so Darius cries out (*z'q*) to Daniel, the Daniel executed (or so he imagines) for the suspicion of treason.

In Darius's lament, the term "living God" is rather unexpected. It is possible, of course, that during the night the king has experienced a religious conversion—unreported by the narrator. (But why then speak of "*your* god"?). Rather more likely, Darius uses the term because of the impression Daniel's religious fidelity has made on him. Darius would never have known of this god save for the fact of Daniel's determined servanthood to the god. If Daniel is willing to die for this god, this god must indeed be worthy, indeed, a "living God."

When Daniel speaks (for the first time in the story) from the pit of death—which comes, no doubt, as a surprise to the king—he also uses language of life:

> "O King, live forever! My god sent his angel and he shut the mouths of the lions. They could not harm me because I was found to be innocent before him and also before you, O King. I have done no harmful act." (6:21 [22])

At this point in the story, many analogies between what has been going on inside the pit and what has been going on outside the pit become apparent. As Darius has sealed the *mouth* of the pit, so God has shut the *mouths* of the lions. During the night, Darius has not been able to eat; likewise, neither have the lions. The lions are not allowed to *harm* Daniel because Daniel has done nothing to *harm* the king.[3]

Daniel's dual allegiance to both God and king is expressed in his language. While Darius refers to Daniel's god as the "living God," Daniel immediately says that his king, too, "lives forever." Daniel is anxious to convince the king that he is innocent not only before his god and but also before his king. He is innocent, he claims, not because he has not broken the edict—that transgression is undeniable—but because he has done nothing that would harm the king. The fact that he has not harmed the king is, he explains to Darius, the reason why the lions have not harmed him.

When, in the next verse, the narrator reports to the reader Daniel's removal from the pit, the narrator clarifies the situation: No harm is found upon Daniel, not because he was faithful to his king, but "because he was faithful to his god."[4]

After Daniel is brought up from the lion pit, the king issues a command and Daniel's accusers are thrown in—they, their children, and their wives. Those who had "eaten the pieces" of Daniel are themselves torn to pieces and eaten by the lions.

This folkloristic "overkill"—to use Sibley Towner's pun (1984:86)—goes beyond "poetic" justice and has been problematic for many interpreters, starting with the Septuagint which confines the punishment to the two other ministers. Norman Porteous (91) comments: "The author of our book had not learnt everything that God had to teach about the nature of justice." Another way of reading the execution, however, is that it says less about the author than it does about the king who orders it and, perhaps, Daniel who raises no hand stop or at least temper it.

Darius's motives for this mass execution are ambiguous. Does he give this command to establish justice for Daniel? Or do personal reasons motivate this drastic action? After all, the men have subverted his power; but, more than that, they have made a fool of him. Darius never takes responsibility for his part in Daniel's entrapment; he never acknowledges that his own gullibility, his own pride, and perhaps his own suspicion of Daniel have contributed to what has happened. By placing all the blame on the officials and by obliterating them and their families, Darius not only punishes the criminals, but he also rids himself of any reminder of his own stupidity.

As for Daniel—obviously Daniel is no longer in the business of rescuing the innocent as he was in chapter 2. He allows the blameless to die with the guilty. His religious conscience may move him to make a stand for his god in the face of political power, but it does not move him in the face of political power to protect fellow human beings.[5]

An Ordinance Forever: Verses 25-28 [26-29]

The "rite of passage" pattern which appeared in chapters 1, 3, and 4 may be discerned here in chapter 6 as well. Daniel is separated from society, sent down to the pit of death, and then brought back among the living. Just as in chapter 3, this rite of passage brings about no change in the one who undergoes it. In chapter 3, the king is the one who is transformed by the experience; so, too, in this present story the king is changed, at least to some extent, by the experience. Of course, we might see in the parallel experiences of Darius and Daniel that the king, too, undergoes a rite of passage. He separates himself from society, spends a sleepless night fasting, and regains his happiness when he finds Daniel safe.

The primary change that takes place here, however, is a change in culture or in societal structure. After witnessing Daniel's survival, Darius passes new legislation ordering that "in all the rule of my kingdom, there is to be trembling and fearing before the god of Daniel" (vs. 26 [27]).[6] This decree ironically cancels out the king's original edict that there be no petitions made to anyone other than the king for thirty days. The law that is not to change changes with the stroke of a pen. Thus, we see that the king's struggle in verse 15 had not so much to do with whether or not the king *could* save Daniel, but whether or not he *should*.[7]

While Darius's second decree reconstitutes society, its relationship to the first decree undermines the reconstitution of society. To begin with, the second, like the first, legislates religious allegiance. Daniel's transgression shows the first to be ineffective. The second is just as likely to be ineffective. There will always be a Daniel, a Shadrach, a Meshach, an Abednego who will show fidelities other than the ones that are legislated.

In the second place, both decrees also legislate political allegiance: the first explicitly, the second implicitly. The first edict makes the king the focus of allegiance; the second makes the god of Daniel the focus of allegiance.

> "I issue a decree that in all the rule of my kingdom there is to be trembling and fearing before the god of Daniel,
> for he is the living God
> and established forever.
> His kingdom is one which cannot be harmed
> and his rule is until the end.
> He delivers and he rescues;
> he works signs and wonders
> in heaven and in earth.
> For he delivered Daniel from the hand of the lions."
> (6:26-27 [27-28])

This god is not called YHWH Elohim, the Most High, or the God, Lord, or King of heaven. This god is represented by and defined by Daniel. The power of this god is manifested in Daniel's very existence ("for he delivered Daniel from the power of the lions"). To worship Daniel's god is to align oneself politically with Daniel. The king's original intent to place Daniel over the kingdom is implicitly fulfilled in the edict that all worship Daniel's god. Consequently, the society at the story's end is not so very different from the society at its beginning.

The ease with which Darius replaces one law with another produces further irony. The passing of law is the attempt to establish permanence, but the fact that one can make a law points to impermanence. What is to keep Darius from replacing this latter law with yet another law insisting upon the worship of yet another god? Even supposing Darius does not change the law, what is to keep some other king from changing it?[8]

One might interpret this striving for permanence, in spite of all its confessional trappings, as bordering on blasphemy.[9] When the worship of a god is established by the law, then the law out-powers the deity. The law inspires the fear that the deity itself cannot. God is reduced to an ordinance and this is indeed how the language of Darius's decree plays: The word he uses to declare that the god of Daniel is *established* forever—namely, *qayyam*—is reminiscent of the language used earlier (vs. 7 [8] and cf. also vs. 15 [16]) to speak of establishing (*leqayyamah*) an *ordinance*—namely, *qeyam*). But for the slight change of a vowel one might read that the god of Daniel is an ordinance forever! As the text stands, the language merely plays with us, but the question remains, What then is really god—deity, legality, or monarchy?

Finally, Darius's decree that all fear and tremble before the god of Daniel collapses the two "laws" that, in the beginning of the story, the conspirators seek to set at odds. The conspirators realize that they will find no complaint against Daniel unless they find it "concerning the law of his god." Their trap is designed to pit the law of Daniel's god against the law of his king. In the end, the two laws are essentially one: The king's law embraces the law of Daniel's god.

Daniel's allegiance to the law of his god is what brings about his downfall; conversely, "the law of his god" confirms his return to power. Not only is the law of Daniel's god portrayed in utilitarian terms, but as long as Daniel's survival and success image the power of his god, then, by the fact of sheer visibility, Daniel himself will always eclipse Daniel's god. After all, what is the result of Darius's legislation?—That everyone converts to the worship of the Most High God and declares this god ultimate sovereign? No. The result of Darius's legislation is that *Daniel prospers*. The legislative enforcement of Daniel's religion sets him up for life.

> Thus Daniel prospered in the kingdom of Darius and in the kingdom of Cyrus the Persian. (6:28 [29])

Chapter Seven

THE BOOK OF DANIEL

ENVISIONING SOVEREIGNTY

Part One
Daniel's Dreams: Chapters 7-12

As we begin the second half of the book, we learn that Daniel, too, has had some unusual dreams and visions during his tenure in court. The first two (chapters 7 and 8) occur during the reign of Belshazzar, presumably before the events of chapter 5. The third (chapter 9) is contemporary with chapter 6, taking place during the reign of Darius. The last (chapters 10-12) occurs at the end of Daniel's career during the reign of Cyrus. The temporal settings of the visions mark them as expansions of the plot. Some visions take us back in Daniel's career, some move us forward; but they all continue to reveal character and to sustain political themes.

Like the dreams of Nebuchadnezzar (chapters 2 and 4), Daniel's visions resemble each other. They play like a fugue with a recurring theme. Beasts/kings rise up in succession, claiming sovereignty and rebelling against God and God's representatives. The succession of monarchs culminates each time with a particularly insolent and destructive figure.

In the First and Third Years of Belshazzar

In the first dream (chapter 7) four monstrous beasts rise from the sea one after another. The fourth beast, especially terrifying, grows a series of horns. The last horn, a small one, has human eyes and speaks arrogant things. With its appearance, a divine court comes to order. The "Ancient of Days" takes his seat, the books are opened, and the horned beast is sentenced and executed. Then, as Daniel watches, a seemingly human creature ("one like a son of man") is presented to the Ancient One and is given everlasting sovereignty over all people.

Daniel, troubled by what he has seen, approaches one of those attending the Ancient One and asks the meaning of all this. The attendant offers an interpretation but, like Daniel interpreting the king's dream in chapter 2, he vastly underreads the vision. The four beasts, he explains, are four kings that will come to power. The holy ones of the Most High, however, will be given the kingdom and possess it forever.

Dissatisfied with the brevity of the answer, Daniel persists. What about the fourth beast and the pompous little horn? This beast, he is told, is a kingdom more terrible than the others. Its horns are kings, the final horn/king the worst of all, speaking blasphemy against the Most High and wearing down the holy ones. He will attempt "to change the times and the law" and for a while he will have power over them. Then the court will sit in judgment and his rule will be taken away. Everlasting kingship will be given to the people of the holy ones of the Most High.

Here the dream ends with Daniel afraid and brooding over what he has seen.

Two years later Daniel has a second dream (chapter 8) much like the first. The principal actors, again, are beasts, but rather than mythical and monstrous, this time they are domesticated. A mighty ram and a he-goat engage in combat. The he-goat is victorious but, in the height of its power, its horn is broken. In the great horn's place grow four more horns and from one of them comes another, a little horn that grows great toward the south and east, rising as high as the heavens. It throws down some of the stars, tramples them, and even raises itself up against the "prince of the host," overthrowing his sanctuary and taking away his burnt offering. The horn casts "truth to the ground" and continues to prosper in all that it does.

A holy one in the dream asks the question on Daniel's mind: How long will this desolation continue? Two thousand, three hundred days, comes the answer. Then the sanctuary will be restored.

Daniel tries in vain to comprehend the vision. A human-like figure named Gabriel ("man of God") appears, having been assigned the task of helping him understand. Frightened, Daniel falls to the ground. The vision, says Gabriel, is of (or for) the time of the end. Daniel, prostrate, falls into a stupor. Gabriel strikes him and stands him on his feet.[1] "Listen," he says (we might suspect impatiently), "and I will inform you of what will happen in the time of fury for it is for the appointed time of the end." He explains to Daniel that the ram with the two horns represents the kings of Media and Persia. The he-goat is the king of Greece with its horns representing a succession of rulers. At the end of the succession, a particularly powerful and destructive king will rise and destroy the people of the holy ones. He will, says Gabriel, even attack the "Prince of princes." But, Daniel is assured, this king will be broken by some mysterious means.

As a result of this disclosure, Daniel falls ill and remains so several days. By his own admission he continues to be bewildered by what he has seen.

The setting of these visions during the reign of Belshazzar lends further irony and depth to the scenario in chapter 5. What might these visions have to do with Daniel's behavior at Belshazzar's feast?

In chapter 5 we saw a bold Daniel confronting a weak and frightened king. Here, oddly enough, we find a frightened Daniel. In fact, Daniel's fear is described in much the same terms as Belshazzar's had been (7:15, 28; 8:17, 27; cf. 5:6, 9, 10). The supercilious Daniel of Belshazzar's banquet shows himself to be tentative, uncertain, and even confused in the face of his own visions. Could the public Daniel be compensating for private insecurities? Or could it be that, in time, Daniel is able to interpret the visions in a way that suits him and reassures him?

Both visions lead up to an arrogant "little" horn who raises himself against God by desolating God's sanctuary. Although Gabriel tells Daniel that the vision is of the time of the end (8:17, 19, 26), Daniel himself confesses that he is confused by what he has seen and that he does not understand it (8:27). After all, one might interpret the end to be occurring rather soon (8:14). Is Belshazzar, for Daniel, an arrogant little horn at work, raising himself against God by desecrating the temple vessels (cf. 5:23)? Daniel has been told that the arrogant one will be broken "but not by human hands" (8:25). Might Daniel see this referring to the hand that writes upon the wall? Is this not the hand that, according to Daniel, holds Belshazzar's very breath (5:23)?

In the second vision Daniel finds himself in the capital city of Susa in the province of Elam. Susa, however, is not the Babylonian capital, where we might have expected him to be. It is, rather, the Persian capital. Daniel's acknowledgment of Susa as the capital suggests imminent political change. At the time of his confrontation with Belshazzar, he is already anticipating the approaching Medes and Persians.

Consequently, when Daniel comes before Belshazzar, he is a man who has had visions of his own, visions that he has not understood, but which nevertheless influence his perception of Belshazzar. Perhaps these visions are what empower Daniel to challenge the king with such disdain. He knows that the capital of the Medes and Persians is established and waiting. He has seen the divine court assembled. He has heard the sentence passed. He merely announces God's judgment upon the king. No matter to Daniel that it is the wrong king. As far as Daniel is concerned, Belshazzar fits the description. He has "lifted [him]self against the Lord of heaven" (5:23), his kingdom is to be "broken," that is, divided between the Medes and Persians (5:28), and he himself will die suddenly and mysteriously (5:30; cf. 8:25: "not by human hands").

In the First Year of Darius

In chapter 6 we saw Daniel, Darius's favorite, making daily petition toward Jerusalem. Here in chapter 9 we hear the content of such petition. Daniel has been reading the prophet Jeremiah who predicted that Jerusalem would lie in ruins for seventy years. Motivated by concern for the city's restoration, Daniel prays a long prayer of supplication. We do not know how much time has passed in the story world since Nebuchadnezzar's capture of Jerusalem, but clearly Daniel feels it is time to remind God of the city's condition. Perhaps, too, he thinks that, with the arrogant Belshazzar now gone, it is time for the holy ones to regain dominion.

The prayer embodies the theology implicit at the beginning of the book. Daniel knows that his God has given Jerusalem over to its enemies. He also assumes that the reasoning of the "old story" is true: God has turned against the people because of their sin. God, according to Daniel, was entirely justified in punishing the people Israel because they had failed to follow God's law. Hence, Daniel confesses the sins of his people, pleading for forgiveness and restoration. In his petition

Daniel does not suggest that the people have been punished enough. Rather, he pleads his case on the basis of God's righteousness (9:7, 14), mercy (9:18), and honor (9:15, 19).

While he is praying on behalf of God's "holy mountain," Gabriel appears to him again in a vision. Gabriel has been sent, he declares, to give Daniel wisdom and understanding. The explanation he gives, however, is far from clear and we are not told whether Daniel truly understands it.

Whereas Daniel, following Jeremiah, has believed that seventy years must pass before Jerusalem would be restored, Gabriel announces that seventy weeks is the accurate time frame. We assume (as most scholars do) that Gabriel means seventy weeks *of years*, but we do not know whether or not Daniel understands this to be the case. Daniel could easily be thinking that the restoration could be very soon.

Seven weeks will pass, proclaims Gabriel, before an anointed prince will appear. Then, during the next sixty-two weeks, the city will be rebuilt but amidst much trouble. At the end of that time, another prince shall come, the anointed one will be brought down, and the city and sanctuary will again be destroyed. For half a week, this intruder is to interrupt the regular sacrifices and offerings, and replace them with desolating abominations until the decreed end comes upon him.

Thus the vision abruptly stops. (We might even wonder if it is at this point that the conspiring officials interrupt Daniel and report him to King Darius.) We are not told Daniel's reaction nor whether he comprehends what he has heard.

If he understands that Gabriel is speaking of many years hence, perhaps he is disheartened at the thought of waiting. If he misunderstands Gabriel's time frame, perhaps he is speechless at the thought of so much happening so quickly. The mention of the desolator may also give Daniel much to ponder. There are more serious things to come than what Belshazzar has done. Furthermore, Daniel's place in all of this is left in question. He can do nothing but wait and watch.

In the Third Year of Cyrus

In the third year of Cyrus of Persia, yet another vision (chapters 10-12) comes to Daniel. Daniel prefaces this account with the disclosure that he had been mourning before having the vision. For three weeks he had abstained from meat and wine and from grooming himself.

Why has Daniel been mourning? The construction of the visions suggests that his prior vision (chapter 9) has given him cause for grief. He is not happy with what he has seen and heard. Is he grieving because the coming trouble is inevitable? Does he grieve because he will play no part in the restoration of the kingdom? Does he think that his fasting will cause God to have a change of heart and to change the course of history? Daniel has not mildly accepted what he has been told, but has continued to beseech God (10:12). God has responded to Daniel's petition and has sent a final vision to help him understand.

In this vision a linen-clad man with an extraordinary appearance greets Daniel. He has a body like beryl, a face like lightening, eyes like fire, and arms and legs like burnished bronze. His voice sounds like that of a multitude. Just as in his first encounter with Gabriel, Daniel falls into a stupor.

After much encouragement he is revived enough to converse with the strange messenger. The man has been in battle, he reports, with the "prince of the kingdom of Persia." He has left this battle long enough to explain to Daniel what is to happen to his people at the end of time. What follows is a long catalogue of kings rising, making alliances, and defeating one another. At the end of the catalogue there comes a "despicable one" who rises in power not on his own merit but through deceit and intrigue. After a frustrated attempt to defeat the "king of the south," he will turn against the holy covenant, profaning the temple with a particularly offensive atrocity, and wreaking violence against the people of God. This king will set himself above any god and speak untold blasphemies. He will continue to prosper despite his evil. He will conquer vast territory and settle "between the sea and the glorious holy mountain." But, the man says abruptly and vaguely, this king "shall come to his end with none to help him" (11:45).

That will be a time of great distress, warns the man, but Michael, "the great prince" will arise to protect the people. Daniel's people, at least those whose names are written in "the book," will be delivered. Even many who are dead will rise to their respective rewards or punishments. Daniel is charged with keeping the book sealed and the words secret until the end.

Two others appear in the vision and voice the inevitable question: "How long until the end of these wonders?" The man answers mysteriously, "a time, times, and half a time" (12:7). Daniel hears but, understandably, does not understand. "What, sir," he asks, "will be the end of these things?" The man refuses to answer. "Go your way, Daniel," he instructs, "for the words are closed and sealed until the end." The wise will understand, he assures Daniel.

But since Daniel does not understand, we would be surprised if he found these words reassuring. Perhaps even the man himself does not understand. He attempts to be precise: one thousand two hundred and ninety days from the desecration of the temple, he asserts. Or maybe it is one thousand three hundred and thirty five days—he cannot be sure. Anyway, Daniel is not to worry about it. "Go your way to the end," says the man. "You shall rest and stand in your allotted place at the end of the days" (12:13).

Part Two
Politics Human and Divine

Two major themes run throughout the book: the political advancement of the Judean hero and the growing recognition of the god of the Judean exiles as the sovereign of sovereigns. These two themes correlate with the fact that only two characters survive the whole of the book: Daniel and God.

The Politics of Daniel

Throughout the first half of the book, particularly chapters 2-6, the narrative focus has been on the characters of the foreign kings. They are the ones who have shown depth and development. Daniel, on the other hand, has been a somewhat synthetic character, a character too wise, too knowledgeable, too faithful to be true. He understands all the mysteries with which he is confronted. He makes no mistakes. He is the epitome of self-confidence. We do not even know if he ever has second thoughts about anything, because we are rarely ever told what he thinks.

There is, however, some subtle development in Daniel's character and that of his alter ego, the collective threesome Shadrach, Meshach, and Abednego. As their positions in the kingdom change, so their characters continue to form.

The Sage's Career

We have watched the Judean exile climb the political ladder from captive prisoner to initiate to sage (chapter 1) to chief sage (chapter 2) to administrator over the province of Babylon (chapters 2-3) to the king's personal adviser (chapter 4) to third ruler in the kingdom (chapter 5) to the prime minister whose appointment over the whole kingdom (6:5 [6]), though delayed, is implied by the end of chapter 6. Even the mention of Daniel's prosperity during the reign of Cyrus (6:28 [29]) could suggest that Cyrus's decision to let the Jews return home was influenced by none other than Daniel.

This theme of political advancement extends into chapter 7, albeit in a more general strain. The interpreter of Daniel's vision promises that "the people of the holy ones of the Most High" will receive "the kingdom and the rule and the greatness of the kingdoms under the whole heaven" (vs. 27; cf. also vss. 18, 22). Daniel surely sees himself as one of that number.

The sage wins political promotion through deception (chapter 1), cooperation (chapters 2, 4, 6) and conflict (chapters 3, 5) with his liege. In every story in Daniel 1-6, the sage is called upon to hold to values that somehow oppose the existent political authority. The story of deception in chapter 1 lays the groundwork for the remaining stories. The young Judeans, by refusing to eat the indenturing food from the king's table, affirm that, though they are willing to serve the king, the source of their wisdom and the subject of their ultimate fidelity is their god, not their king. In this story and those that follow, the sages show themselves ready to oppose political power for higher values—whether by speaking the truth about an unpleasant dream or vision (chapters 2, 4, 5) or by disobeying the command to pay ultimate allegiance to some king who thinks his sovereignty supreme (chapters 1, 3, 6).

The irony involved in all of this courageous resistance, however, is that every instance of resistance to political authority, every affirmation of priorities other than the priority of political power is rewarded—how?—with the bestowal of more political power. When we look at the overall picture of Daniel, the so highly valued piety and wisdom of our Judean heroes become means to political ends. The world of Daniel is a world of political ambition. While our Judean sages busily assist the Most High in teaching lessons to the kings concerning the ways in which pride corrupts the powerful, the sages themselves are consistently being promoted to positions of greater power.

In the final analysis, political power is not just the concern of kings, but it is also the concern of the Judean sage. The fact that Daniel becomes ever more like a king is seen not only from the pattern of his political advancement, but also from the narrative structure.

Daniel and Nebuchadnezzar

In chapter 6 Daniel's experiences are very similar to those of his old friend Nebuchadnezzar in chapter 4. The king's troubles are precipitated by a decree from the holy ones, Daniel's by a decree from the king. Both decrees involve the recognition of sovereignty. In both stories, after learning of the decree, the protagonists go to similar places and say and do things that bring about their respective sentences. Nebuchadnezzar goes up to the roof of his palace; Daniel goes up to an upper room in his house. Nebuchadnezzar looks out over Babylon; Daniel looks toward Jerusalem. Nebuchadnezzar praises himself and his accomplishments; Daniel makes petition before his god—a petition, chapter 9 would lead us to believe, concerning the religious (9:24) *and political* (9:25) restoration of Jerusalem. In chapter 4, a voice from heaven interrupts Nebuchadnezzar and the decree is fulfilled; in chapter 6, the officials interrupt Daniel and the edict is enforced.

Both protagonists, on being sentenced, suffer the loss of their political position and are forced into the company of beasts. The king is driven from society; Daniel is thrown into the pit. Nebuchadnezzar exists with the wild beasts; Daniel passes the night with the lions. Nebuchadnezzar is fed the food of beasts; Daniel is to be the food of beasts. Nebuchadnezzar is delivered because he acknowledges the Most High; Daniel is delivered because he is faithful. Both protagonists are restored: Nebuchadnezzar is reestablished upon his throne with even more greatness than before; Daniel is restored to royal favor, and Daniel's god and Daniel as divine representative enjoy the respect that was to be bestowed, at the beginning of the story, only upon the king.

Two Doxologies

A common vocabulary shared by the two stories broadens the parallel. The language that Nebuchadnezzar uses in his first doxology in 4:1-3 [3:31-33] is echoed by Darius at the end of chapter 6. Both kings address their messages to "all peoples, nations and languages who dwell in all the earth." Both use the common expression "May your peace be multiplied" to greet their subjects. Both praise God's signs and wonders. Both speak of the endurance of God's kingdom and rule.

Both of these doxologies with their common vocabulary occur at strategic transitional places in the overarching literary structure.

Nebuchadnezzar's first doxology (4:1-3 [3:31-33]) is ambiguously placed.[2] On first reading, it looks as though it concludes the story in chapter 3, just as Darius's doxology concludes chapter 6. In fact, because chapters 3 and 6 are so similar, a closing doxology on the part of Nebuchadnezzar in chapter 3 would be just as appropriate as Darius's closing hymn in chapter 6. Both kings have just witnessed the miraculous deliverance of their Judean administrators; and both kings are impressed by the power of this god.[3] Of course, we have seen that Nebuchadnezzar's doxology also functions as the introduction to chapter 4. This doxology, then, like the transitional sentence in 5:31 [6:1] ("And Darius the Mede took/received the kingdom . . ."), readily closes one story while opening another.

When we turn to Darius's doxology with this earlier passage in mind we may see a similar function. Though Darius's proclamation obviously closes chapter 6, it also looks ahead to chapter 7. In opening chapter 4, Nebuchadnezzar's doxology is followed by a first person account of a flashback: The king tells of having a night vision and of someone (Daniel/Belteshazzar) coming to interpret it. Darius's doxology is remarkably similar: It is followed (though not immediately) by a flashback to the days of Belshazzar, by Daniel's first person account of a night vision and someone coming to interpret it.

The analogies are striking. Both men are "troubled" (4:5 [2]; 7:15, 28). Both visions are about kings being overthrown. Both contain judgments or decrees from heaven (4:17 [14], 24 [21]; 7:10, 26). Both contain subsequent doxologies uttered by the one having the vision (4:34-35 [31-32]; 7:14; cf. also the interpreter's doxology, 7:27). Both doxologies describe the enduring nature of God's kingdom, the everlasting nature of God's rule. In both accounts there is a reference to "all peoples, nations and languages." In both accounts kings are anomalous beasts: In chapter 7 four kings as beasts with the characteristics of various animals rise from the sea. In chapter 4 Nebuchadnezzar becomes like a beast, dwelling with the beasts of the field and eating grass, yet also resembling a bird with long feathers and claws. In both accounts divine judgment is passed upon a king because of what he says (4:29-31 [26-28]; 7:8, 11, 20, 25-26). Furthermore, in neither chapter can the visionary interpret his own vision; someone else must explain it to him.

Daniel and the Kingdom

Throughout the stories of Daniel in chapters 1-6, signs and wonders (visions and deliverances) have taken place for the benefit of the king. The Judean sages have functioned as agents who assist in bringing new knowledge to the king. Starting with chapter 7, however, the visions are for Daniel's benefit. He is never told to report what he has seen to any of the kings. If anything, he is told to keep what he has seen to himself. It is as though Daniel becomes a full-fledged character as the stories end and the visions begin. Daniel takes over what the narratives (chapters 2, 4, 5) have set up as the king's role. Now it is Daniel rather than the king who sees images of the fantastic, the anomalous, the bizarre, images of greatness established and greatness fallen.

The visions of hubris and the miraculous deliverances have revealed to the kings the limitations of their power. So, too, Daniel is reminded in the vision of chapter 7 that foreign power is limited and temporary. The kingdom will not always belong to the beasts; someday it will be given to the people of the holy ones of the Most High. Does Daniel not also count himself among these, the people who are to receive the kingdom? As a person faithful to his god, why should he not also participate in the coming kingdom of his god and people? In fact, might it not occur to him that the "one like a son of man" to whom will be given control of the kingdom will be none other than Daniel himself? After all, he is of royal, or at least noble, seed. And who has more wisdom and political expertise than Daniel? Besides, why should God send such visions to Daniel specifically if not to ready him for the coming kingdom?

We can imagine that Daniel fully expects to participate in the establishment of God's kingdom and—what is equivalent in Daniel's mind—in the physical, religious, and political restoration of Jerusalem (chapter 9). As we reflect on chapters 1-6, we see, on the surface, an extended story about how one can be a faithful Jew and, at the same time, be politically successful—a story about, in Humphreys's terms, "a life-style for the diaspora." But we might also see that complementary interests can also be compromised interests. While Nebuchadnezzar on his roof praises Babylon, Daniel in his upper chamber prays for (chapter 9) and toward Jerusalem. The reader might ask, Can he pay equal allegiance to Babylon and Jerusalem? Can he be completely faithful to his king when harboring political aspirations of his own?

We might see that when a person is trying, not just to survive, but to succeed in a foreign political system, religious allegiance may also be a prime candidate for compromise. How easy it is to underread divine judgment (chapters 2 and 4) when facing a violent and temperamental king! How easy it is to overread divine judgment (chapter 5) when insulted by a weak, childish king who is about to be overthrown anyway! Moreover, by the end of his career, we learn that Daniel "prospers" during the reign of Cyrus (6:28) and we suspect by the reference to "rich food," "meat," and "wine" (10:3), that Daniel has no qualms about eating from King Cyrus's hand. Daniel's youthful idealism (chapter 1) has dwindled to the point where Daniel serves and benefits from a king who is his god's enemy (10:13, 20)![4]

A politically aspiring Daniel may also inform the way we understand his behavior during his visions. Not only is he preoccupied with the question of "How long, O Lord?" (cf. chapter 9 and 12:6), but he faints or grows ill seemingly whenever he is told that his visions of a restored kingdom will come to pass in "the time of the end," "many days hence" (cf. 8:17-18, 26-27; 10:14-15), rather than in his own lifetime. The vision of chapter 7 allows his political hopes to be sustained, but with each vision that follows, his chances for active political involvement diminish. Increasingly, Daniel seems unable to understand what is actually being shown to him.[5] It is not until the very end of the book that Daniel receives any sort of assurance of his role in the kingdom: "Go your way till the end, and you shall rest, and shall stand in your allotted place at the end of the days" (12:13). Whether or not this answer satisfies Daniel, we are not told.

Daniel and Wisdom

Daniel's obvious and somewhat impotent struggle to understand his visions reveals a more poignant limitation as far as his character is concerned—the limitation of his wisdom. As his story progresses, Daniel becomes increasingly self-assured in matters of wisdom and interpretation. From the ending of chapter 2, he allows his wisdom and abilities to be praised without disclaimer. He interprets and advises seemingly without assistance. But, lest we become too enamored of Daniel and his ability, the narrator shows us another side of him. Beginning with chapter 7, Daniel becomes a much more complex character. We are finally allowed inside Daniel's head and what we find is that Daniel is not as infallible or as self-confident as he seems.

He is like Nebuchadnezzar who dreams and is troubled. He is like Belshazzar who sees visions and is afraid. He is like the other sages who are powerless to discern divine communication. The sage who would interpret the dreams and visions of others cannot interpret his own.

Indeed the reader suspects that the visions recur like a refrain because God cannot be sure that Daniel understands what he is being told. The visions move from the enigmatic to the specific and familiar, from monsters and grandiose theophanies to domesticated rams and goats to mundane descriptions of particular kings and events. Despite the shift toward more candid and common communication, we are still never certain that Daniel comprehends.

Ironically, in the last vision, a bewildered Daniel is told that "the wise will understand" (12:10), that "the wise will shine like the bright sky" (12:3). But who can truly be "wise" about the time of the end? The messenger himself does not seem to know when it will come (12:11-12; cf. 8:14). As for Daniel, he is charged with keeping all this a secret. He is to seal up the book until the time of the end (12:4). Daniel, however, has given a full account in a book open for all to see. Did he grow weary waiting for the end? Or were the visions simply vague enough for any time to look like the end?[6]

The Sovereignty of God

Divine Visibility

In the first part of the book, we recognized the foreign king to be the major character. We have also seen some more intricate development in the character of Daniel. God, on the other hand, has hardly been a character at all. Except for direct action in chapter 1 (God "gives" Jerusalem to Nebuchadnezzar, "gives" favor and compassion to Daniel before the chief eunuch, and "gives" knowledge and wisdom to Daniel and his friends), God stays behind the scenes—a certain but untouchable, unobservable presence. Throughout the book God has communicated through dreams and visions. With the exception of a brief appearance in chapter 7, God, for the most part, remains decidedly invisible, using quasi-divine spokespersons to relay and interpret divine messages. It is precisely God's invisibility that constructs the conflict concerning sovereignty.

Political power is not merely a human goal in the world of Daniel.

Political power is God's concern as well. Consider how God demonstrates divine sovereignty in this book. With the signs and wonders God brings down the mighty and delivers the troubled. In the world of Daniel, however, God deals only with politically important people. God only deposes and delivers people who have political authority (kings [chapter 4], administrators [chapter 3], prime ministers [chapter 6]). Why?

Because in order for people to believe in divine sovereignty, the divine sovereign has to have high visibility. It does not count to simply whisk the heroes away, to deliver them to another world, so to speak. It does not count to depose kings without an explanation of why they are being deposed and who is bringing this about. In order to be effective, God's action must have witnesses—and the more politically prestigious the witness, the more wonderful the sign, the more significant the wonder. Perception is everything. An anonymous god who does anonymous work is no god at all. Religion cannot cope with secret sovereigns.[7]

Divine Recognition

Thus we come to the second of the themes which crescendo through the story: the recognition of the god of the Judean exiles as the sovereign of sovereigns. From chapter 1 in which the king is totally unaware of this god, the kings come to know of, and increasingly affirm, the Most High. At the end of chapter 2, Nebuchadnezzar says, while paying homage and offering incense to Daniel,

> "Truly your god is a god of gods and a lord of kings and a revealer of mysteries that you are able to reveal this mystery" (2:47).

At the end of chapter 3, the king not only affirms the god but legislates against blasphemy:

> "Therefore I make a decree that any people, nation, or language that says anything amiss against the god of Shadrach, Meshach, and Abednego shall be dismembered, and their houses laid in ruins; because there is no other god who is able to deliver like this." (3:29)

In chapter 4 the king makes a personal confession of belief in the power of this god who has shown sovereignty over the sovereign and who, consequently, is appropriately entitled the "Most High" (4:37 [34]) and the "king of heaven" (4:34 [31]). The confession of chapter 4, while not legislative, is couched in the form of a national proclamation:

> "Now I, Nebuchadnezzar, praise and extol and glorify the king of heaven for all his works are right and his ways are just . . . ." (4:34 [31])

By the time we reach the end of chapter 6, Darius's legislation is even more stringent than the legislation of chapter 3:

> "I make a decree that in all my royal rule, everyone will tremble and fear before the god of Daniel . . . ." (6:26 [27])

In each of these proclamations, God is defined relationally. God is given no personal name (cf. Davies 1986:81-88). God is the god of Daniel or the god of Shadrach, Meshach, and Abednego. Even Nebuchadnezzar's use of the apellatives "Most High" and "king of heaven" reflect a relational understanding: Nebuchadnezzar is "high"—that we have learned from the image of the great tree. He reaches to heaven and he is, obviously, king. The god who has brought him down, however, is "higher" than he. Anyone whose might is greater than Nebuchadnezzar's is indeed "king of heaven."

From this naming, then, we may see how the divine is understood in the story world of Daniel. Except in chapter 1, God is not a character whom we see and hear. God's presence is always mediated: Characters report it, holy ones and heavenly voices represent it, sages interpret it, kings confess it and legislate the recognition of it; but the presence of God is not visible in the form of a distinct, divine character. We know what we know of God by watching what happens to the human characters, and in the case of Daniel, it is difficult to keep from fusing divine and human, as we see from Nebuchadnezzar's treatment of Daniel at the end of chapter 2.

Like the decree before it, the decree of Darius (6:26 [27]) that everyone is to worship the god of Daniel is (since it is an edict established by the king) one that "cannot be changed according to the law of the Medes and Persians which will not pass away" (6:8 [9]; cf. 12 [13] and 15 [16]). Just as the identity of God is confined by relational terms, so the sovereignty of God is limited by the royal legislation. The legislation that confers the recognition of sovereignty controls the recognition of sovereignty.

Having the god of Daniel recognized in the legislation of a powerful regime like that of the Medes and Persians is indeed impressive and suggests, of course, that the recognition of the sovereignty of the Most High, because it is now law, will never pass away. But the *law* of the Medes and Persians is one that will not pass away only as long as the *rule* of the Medes and the Persians does not pass away. When the rule of the Medes and Persians passes away, then so does the law—and so does the recognition of the sovereignty of the Most High. Thus, the world of Daniel contains an ironic circle of sovereignty. God may establish kings and kingdoms and "allow them to pass away" (2:21; 4:31 [28]; 5:20), but when they "pass away," God must start again the struggle to gain recognition. In other words, human sovereignty depends upon divine sovereignty, and conversely, divine sovereignty is dependent upon the recognition of human sovereigns.[8]

At least Daniel 7 discerns the maddening circle. Daniel's first vision is a vision of a world in which the cycle will be broken. A kingdom will finally be established in which the sovereignty of God is not dependent upon the attitudes of human monarchs, but is immediately recognized by everyone. The one who is "ancient of days" will become a visible presence. A kingdom will finally be established that really does have legislative authority. As can be seen in the court scene in Daniel 7, divine and human sovereigns will be put in their rightful places: The divine will be passing legislation concerning the human and not vice versa. The legislation of this kingdom is indeed what the legislation of human kingdoms cannot be: It is the law that cannot pass away, the divine decree that cannot be changed—it is written and sealed in the book (Daniel 12:1, 4, 9).[9]

But the circle is no sooner halted than it starts again. There must be "one like a son of man," a Gabriel, a Michael, an anointed prince, holy ones to take care of the business of the kingdom or, theologically speaking, to mediate the presence of God. The "fire" of God cannot immediately and constantly be borne. The kingdom is handed back to the people—the people of the holy ones of the Most High.

Even attempts to keep the struggle on the divine plane eventually fail to make an impact. God's supposed defeat of the arrogant one is described with increasing vagueness. In the first vision God, "the Ancient of Days," appears to put an end to the arrogant one. He is sentenced and executed, "burned with fire" (7:11). In the subsequent visions, however, God does not appear. The arrogant figure continues to prosper in what it does (8:12) and there is only a promise that, after a certain time, things will be set right (8:14; 9:27; 12:1-13).

A judge with white clothing and hair, a throne of fire, and thousands in attendance, a beast that is put to death and burned as if it were a holocaust—this we can visualize. But from this dazzling scene of swift justice we move to muddy assurances: "he shall be broken but not by human hands" (8:25), "the decreed end [will be] poured out upon the desolator" (9:27), "he shall come to his end with none to help him" (11:45). As the visions recur they fail to rouse our imagination—we cannot envision what the end might look like. Their repetition prevents closure. Every time we think the conflict is resolved, it merely starts again. Even where the words stop on the page, we find no completion nor certainty (12:11-12)—only the encouragement to wait (12:13). We find ourselves losing confidence that God's sovereignty will finally, definitively, win out.

The Endless Circle

The ultimate irony in the book of Daniel, then, is that the kingdom as Daniel envisions it—whether mediated or otherwise—never manifests itself. The events that are decreed to take place in "the time of the end" never come to pass. This irony is, conceivably, enmeshed in the political tangle of the Jewish sage and the foreign sovereign. When someone stands up to political authority because of religious values, the reward is more political power. Where there is political power, there is hierarchy. Where there is hierarchy, there is always the threat of corruption—the hierarchy itself becomes god.

Perhaps this is why, in visions of the kingdom, God must sit one throne removed. God's kingdom is perhaps a dangerous metaphor for those who value political power as the most prized form of reward. The envisioned kingdom is not for Daniel to experience. Daniel stands on the brink of the kingdom; he sees it as Moses sees the promised land. But kingdoms, like Canaans, can be corrupted and corrupting. The purity of the kingdom is preserved only in its elusiveness.

In the end of Daniel, there is no end. The "end" does not come; the kingdom that will never pass away is not manifested—at least not in the pattern of kingdoms that we have been shown thus far in the book. The promise (decree?) that does stand, however, is that the people of the holy ones, those who turn many to righteousness, the wise ones, will "shine like the stars." Their endurance is the sign of hope; more likely, their endurance is the sign of the kingdom itself.

Just as Daniel's survival of the lions represents the indestructibility of God's kingdom (6:26-27), so too, the people who survive other beastly powers (7:21-22) are manifestations of the kingdom. The beasts who rise from the sea in chapter 7, the ram and the multi-horned he-goat in chapter 8, the king who becomes a beast in chapter 4 all allow us to see Daniel's survival in the lion pit as a paradigm of his survival of exile and oppression. Daniel has survived not only the foreign rulers,[10] but all parties who are jealous of and hostile to him and his friends—to use the text's pun, those who "eat the pieces of" Daniel and his friends. Daniel survives exile just as he survives the lions: He survives because, despite his ambitions and compromises, he is faithful both to God and king.

Likewise, his god and his king survive because he is faithful. Just as kings do not last very long without faithful subjects, neither do gods. As the psalmist says,

> What profit is there in my death,
>   if I go down to the Pit?
> Will the dust praise you?
>   Will it tell of your faithfulness? (Ps 30:9 [10])

God and humanity are interdependent. Daniel understands this well. "Oh my God," he prays,

> "open your eyes and see our desolations and the city that is *called by your name*. . . .Oh Lord, listen and act. Do not delay—*for your own sake,* Oh my God, for your city and your people are *called by your name*! (9:18-19)

Human faithfulness renders God visible. This is why God cannot let the faithful ones completely perish. If God lets Daniel, or the community "called by God's name," perish in exile, or in the midst of any other kind of oppression, what becomes of the sovereignty of the God of Israel?

> Who would proclaim it?
> Who would see it?
> Who would understand?

NOTES

Notes to Chapter One: Eating From the King's Hand

[1]Cf. Jer 25:1 and 2 Chron 36:21 as opposed to 2 Kings 24-25. We cannot depend upon our narrator for historical accuracy. It has been said that a good storyteller remembers the past and hopes that his audience does not.

[2]Lacocque (27) also sees this connection, but concludes from the analogy that the offices for which the young men are being prepared are also priestly in nature. I see, rather, that the phrase "without blemish" raises the thematic issue of sovereignty (god versus king) and plays with the notion of offering or sacrifice. Are these young men being "sacrificed" to the king in the same sense that Jerusalem, King Jehoiakim, and the temple vessels have been given (sacrificed?) to Nebuchadnezzar? At the very least, the play on sacrifice foreshadows chapters 3 and 6.

[3]According to Montgomery (129-30), these names reflect intentional perversions of the names of Babylonian deities: Bel, Marduk, and Nebo. If they are indeed such perversions the narrator may be sharing a joke with the reader behind the characters' backs.

[4]From the root *gʿl* ("abhor") not *gʾl* ("redeem"). The spelling is late. Its other occurrences refer to cultic defilement, cf. Isa 59:3; Lam 4:14; Mal 1:7, 12; Ezra 2:62 = Neh 7:64.

[5]Such is the reading reflected in Ginsberg's argument (1954:256), based on Lev 11:37-38, that the only food that would be beyond defilement is dried legumes; hence the reason for Daniel's later request for vegetables, "seeds." The observation that ritual purity appears to be a prominent concern in the literature of the second temple period—cf. Jub 22:16; Jdt 10:5; 2 Macc 5:27; Tob 1:10—also supports such an understanding of Daniel's situation (see Porteous's discussion, 29-31).

[6]See also Lacocque's observation (28) that food is a symbol of one's culture. He compares Daniel's refusal of the king's food with the more modern situation of immigrants in American and French cities who insist on maintaining their national diet.

[7]The causative (hifil) form of the verb as well as the grammatical construction of the sentence makes two readings possible. Either Daniel simply understands dreams and visions or God gives Daniel understanding.

Notes to Chapter Two: Such Dreams As Kings Are Made Of

[1]The temporal incongruity between chapters 1 and 2 has prompted the common observation that biblical authors and redactors are unconcerned with accurate synchronization. This might stem from a lack of "genuine historical interest" (Porteous, 39), or from lack of care on the redactor's part (Davies 1976: 394). The notes to the standard critical edition of the Masoretic text, *Biblia Hebraica Stuttgartensia*, suggests that the phrase be emended to "the tenth year," but no manuscript or version support is cited for the change.

[2]Davies (1976:393) points out the tension between Daniel's action in this instance and verse 25 where Daniel is introduced to the king as if for the first time.

[3]On "behold" indicating shift in point of view, see Berlin, 62-63.

[4]The succession of kingdoms is an attested motif in ancient Near Eastern literature (see Flusser, Hasel; Swain). While most scholars commenting on Daniel 2 attempt to identify the various metals with a succession of kings, dynasties, or empires (and thus, in a manner of speaking, adopt Daniel's temporal interpretation), a few (though still historically oriented) have been drawn to a more synchronic understanding (e.g. Ginsberg 1948:8; and more recently, Baldwin, 92-94).

[5]Cf. Montgomery's comments on the distinction between the image and the stone. The image is

> . . . the artificial figure of a human body . . . . The metallic character of the Image deliberately stamps it as artifical and but heightens the truth of the symbol. For it is the man-made and hand-made construction of the kingdom of this world that the narrator would portray. The figure stands there stiff and stark, the product of human law and convention at their best and truest, but a lifeless creation. Over against this appears the mobile, supernaturally moving stone, coming how and whence none knows, which, as is true of the cosmic forces, crumples up that proud and complacent work of human art. (187)
>
> The sphere of that Kingdom is that of its predecessors, only it possesses the everlasting endurance of the natural rock. The supernatural feature is that this Stone becomes a great Mountain. The artifice of men's hands has been replaced by the earthly type of eternity. (191)

[6]Hebrew narrators employ dreams as messages from the divine (e.g., Genesis 21), a use much in keeping with a common ancient Near Eastern understanding of dreams (see Oppenheim's classic study), but they also use dreams to indicate mental preoccupation. Joseph's dreams of the sheaves and the stars Genesis 37), for example, are telling reflections of his pompous personality.

[7]Cf. Baldwin's use (92) of Jung in her reading of Daniel 2.

[8]All of these terms are commonly used in the context of cultic ritual. "There can be no question but that Neb[uchadnezzar] intended divine honors to Dan[iel] in the true spirit of Paganism" (Montgomery, 180).

[9]The discrepancy has often been explained by appealing to a reconstructed redactional history (see again Davies 1976). Chapters 1 and 2 represent two originally independent accounts of Daniel's introduction to the Babylonian court that have been secondarily fitted into a chronological framework. The process and the effect is much like that of the two creation stories at the beginning of Genesis—they function to tell the story of the beginning of the world, but they go about it in quite distinctive ways. Their present arrangement lures the reader into viewing them as sequential. (Cf. also the two stories of David's introduction into Saul's court.) Such an analysis may explain how the stories came together, but it does not explain the effect they have.

Notes to Chapter Three: The King's Public Image

[1]The ancient Greek translation (Septuagint), however, does have a temporal introductory clause, "In his eighteenth year." If, as Lacocque (56) suggests, this is borrowed from Jeremiah 52:29, the Greek implies that Nebuchadnezzar's erection of the image is a commemoration of the destruction of Jerusalem and its temple. The word *ḥnk*, "dedicate," also links the image with the temple (cf. 1 Kgs 8:63; 2 Chr 7:5, 9; Ezra 6:16, 17) and the city (cf. Neh 12:17).

[2]This association was made as early as Hippolytus (ii, 15), see the discussion of Montgomery, 195.

[3]"Fall down" and "pay homage" are the words and acts of worship (cf. Dan 2:46). *Sgd* appears only in contexts dealing with the worship of idols (cf. Isa 44:15, 17, 19; 46:6). The noun itself, *ṣelem*, is often used in reference to idols (e.g., 2 Kgs 11:18; Ezek 16:17; Num 33:52) but its usage is not confined to this (e.g., Ps 39:7; 73:20). The nature of the "image" in Daniel 2 is, of course, ambiguous. None of the characters in the story refer to the image as an idol, but the reader is aware that, at least on one level, the image represents the idol of human pride and power.

[4]Cf. Lacocque's comment (59): "The absence of any formal identification is not necessarily a weakness . . . . In any case, the stele represents the empire

and is the manifestation of a grotesque hubris." Montgomery (195; following Jephet Ibn 'Ali, *Commentary on Daniel,* 1889) also regards the image as "a symbol of allegiance to the empire."

[5]Although it is an attempt at historical reconstruction rather than a literary reading, compare Shea's interpretation of this story as the swearing of a loyalty oath after a rebellion during Nebuchadnezzar's reign.

[6]Several scholars have seen the repetitions in this story to have a humorous and/or satirical function (cf. Good, 52; Towner 1984:48; Baldwin, 102.

[7]While the omission of Daniel is understandable from a redactional view of the story's transmission, Daniel's absence is, nonetheless, surprising to the final form reader (cf. Towner's puzzlement, 1984:47). Perhaps, since he passed the provincial post on to his friends (2:49), Daniel was not among those summoned to the gathering and so was not confronted with the crisis. Or we could suppose that the Chaldeans do not implicate Daniel because he is a favorite of the king. Porteous notes that ". . . to bring Daniel into this chapter as worthy of punishment for loyalty to a God whom Nebuchadnezzar, according to the previous chapter, had acknowledged so handsomely, would have seemed very strange" (55). Although Porteous is referring to the narrator's logic, a slightly different version of his observation would fit Nebuchadnezzar's logic. Let us assume from the end of chapter 2 that Nebuchadnezzar is in awe of Daniel's almost superhuman ability. Would he then require this quasi-divine figure to bow to an image whose significance Daniel himself had explained to the king in the first place (assuming that the newly constructed image is based on the image of the dream)? Of course, such a hypothesis leaves a question against Daniel's character since he does nothing to aid his friends. But, then, Shadrach, Meshach, and Abednego are not assertive characters either, they simply respond to the situation that is presented to them.

[8]Lacocque (61) writes: ". . . in reality the accusation is based on facts. What is slanderous is presenting the Jews as poor administrators of the affairs of the kingdom."

[9]Wharton (174-75) puts it nicely:

> [T]his unconditional affirmation of integrity asserts that no threat and no conceivable outcome can deter these witnesses from their commitment to the highest and best that they know. They cannot answer for God in this situation, but they can answer for themselves. From the human side, and *even if that were the only side there is,* they propose to stand their ground.

[10]The grammar of this sentence demands a translation such as, "If he is able, our God whom we serve, to deliver us . . . " (cf. Montgomery, 206; and Lacocque, 62). Translations (e.g. RSV and KJV) which read something along the lines of "If it be so, our God . . . is able . . ." are guided less by grammar than by a theological bias against questioning God's ability (see Coxon 1976).

[11]Our expectation of death might also be controlled by genre. It has been argued that the story displays the characteristics of a martyr legend (see, e.g., Collins, 55; Kuhl, 71-76; Porteous, 55-56). The only clear examples that we have of martyr legends, however, postdate this story. Perhaps it is more accurate to say that our expectations are guided by less formal elements, plot- and theme-oriented allusions and paradigms (see the discussion of allusion and paradigm in the Introduction) or even our common human experience.

[12]Lacocque (66) also observes that, just as the ram is substituted for Isaac, so the executioners are substituted for the three Jews.

[13]The pause is indicated in the Masoretic text by a *pe,* the mark of an open paragraph. Furthermore, when our attention is returned to Nebuchadnezzar in verse 23, it is clear that we have experienced an implicit temporal ellipsis of at least a few minutes (on implicit and explicit ellipses, see Genette, 106-109). At some point a fourth man has joined the original three, the bonds have been loosened, and the men have begun walking around. This activity, however, is not reported, but is later understood to have taken place.

[14]Cf. Lacocque (66): ". . . only the king sees the miracle (vss. 24-25); for the miracle is never seen except by the one whom it concerns . . . ."

[15]Of this Good (52) writes "the thought will not down that the list in v. 27 would have been complete had not some weary copyist decided, 'Oh, to hell with it!' "

[16]Of course, the interpreter has the right to focus on the persecuted's point of view, see, for example, the provocative readings of James Wharton and and Robert McAfee Brown. However, the story itself clearly elevates the oppressor's point of view.

[17]Sternberg (176-79) argues that all biblical narratives are about the acquisition of knowledge about God.

[18]A thorough and innovative treatment of this metaphor can be found in McNutt, chapter 5.

[19]This interpretation on metaphorical grounds is supported by the narrator's collective portrayal of Shadrach, Meshach, and Abednego. The fact that none of these three exhibits an independent personality makes their association with the Jewish nation more apparent.

Notes to Chapter Four: The King's Praises

[1]Of, course, Nebuchadnezzar does not actually break the frame of artistic space, but the ambiguity of his addressee changes the borders, allowing the artistic space to be expanded (cf. Uspensky, 137-40).

[2]The way in which texts confer subjectivity upon their viewers is known, in the field of cinema, as "suture." Silverman (194-236) presents an extensive

theoretical discussion of this phenomenon in her book on semiotics.

[3]By placing this doxology with the preceding story (= 3:31-33 in Aramaic) rather than with Daniel 4, the traditional Masoretic text (e.g., *Biblia Hebraica Stuttgartensia*) attests to its ambiguous relationship to its context.

[4]The meaning of the Aramaic word here (*harhorin*) is uncertain (see Montgomery, 226-27, and Lacocque, 72). Its root may come, according to Montgomery (227) from *hrh*, "to conceive." The word seems to be used in later Rabbinic writings to refer to "impure" dreams. Ibn Ezra speaks of "a mental *harhor* without ejaculation." The sexual connotations do not seem amiss to the post-Freudian reader when one considers the phallic image of the tree (cf. also the gold image in chapter 3!) and its subsequent castration. However one nuances the word, I think it consistent with the story to surmise that the "imaginings" are rather unpleasant.

[5]Slotki (30) observes this forshadowing device. Coxon (1986:96-97) makes an interesting suggestion on the basis of an Arabic etymology that the word is a *double-entendre* that plays upon both the meanings of "flourishing/prosperous" and "foolish/weakminded."

One particular metaphor, Ps 92:12-15 [13-16], in which people are imaged as plants, casts a highly ironic light upon Nebuchadnezzar's statement in Daniel 4:4 [1]. In the psalm the righteous "flourish like the palm tree, and grow like a cedar in Lebanon. They are planted in the house of the Lord; they flourish in the courts of our God." In direct contrast, Nebuchadnezzar, who by Daniel's implication is unrighteous, flourishes in his own house which, as we discover in 4:29-30 [26-27], is more important to him than the house of any deity.

[6]Montgomery (223) was, I think, the first to suggest that the change of person represents more than simply a lapse on the part of the author:

> [I]t has not been observed by the comm. that the same phenomenon appears in the book of Tobit, which begins with the ego of the hero and passes over into the 3d pers. at 3:7 . . . . The change of person in both stories is due to an unconscious dramatic sense. In Tobit the hero speaks in the first act, but when the drama passes to other scenes and characters, the ordinary narrative style of the 3d pers. is adopted. And so in our story, in which the alleged edict form sat lightly on the composer's mind, dramatically the account of the king's madness is told in the 3d pers., for of that he would not have been a sane witness; the change of person is anticipated somewhat too early in v. 16. The dramatic propriety involved appears from the fact that probably most readers do not stumble over the incongruity.

[7]Cf. Montgomery's observation (225): "The story is deftly told. The seer was Daniel to the Jewish readers, but Belteshazzar to the court." On naming as an indicator of perceptual point of view, see Berlin, 59-61.

[8]Gowan (20) recalls that, according to Niebuhr, there are three types of pride: the pride of power, the pride of knowledge, and the pride of virtue. Gowan observes that the Old Testament is barely aware of the last two but is acutely conscious of the first. I think one could legitimately question, however, if in this story (whether the narrator acknowledges it or not) Daniel is not dangerously close to the pride of knowledge. He, at least, now seems to be taking his wisdom for granted and he easily accepts (even divine) credit without disclaimer.

[9]This instance in which the character intends one thing, but God hears another, gives the reader the license of suspicion. We are not required to take Nebuchadnezzar's speech (at this point or any other) at face value.

[10]This theme of dominion—the grasping of it and the loss of it—plays ironically on the theme of the Genesis 1 creation story. There humanity is given dominion over all the birds, fish and beasts. Here in Daniel 4, the one who has seized dominion is one who must become like a bird-beast over which other humans have dominion.

[11]In a sense, the progression of Nebuchadnezzar's recognition of divine sovereignty is very like the plagues and the hardening of Pharaoh's heart in the Exodus story. Not until God strikes the Pharaoh's household with the death of his firstborn son, does Pharaoh relent and allow the people to go.

[12]As many scholars have recognized, both the first-person narrative voice as well as many of the motifs in Daniel 4, are reminiscent of the Nabonidus traditions. Nabonidus's extended absence from Babylon is described in the Harran inscriptions. In the Prayer of Nabonidus, the Most High afflicts the king with a disease that lasts seven years. The text implies that the disease is a result of sins that are remitted by a Jewish exorcist. Daniel 4 shares with the Nabonidus material some basic blocks of tradition, but the blocks, as they stand in Daniel 4, have been reshaped and repainted to produce a very different effect. The absence from Babylon is punishment, not a deity's act of protection. The disease is madness. The sin is hubris. The Jew involved is merely an interpreter not an exorcist. And, of course, the king is Nebuchadnezzar, not Nabonidus. (For a more detailed discussion of the contrasts, see Dupont-Sommer, and Collins 1984:62-3.) The result is a story about sovereignty, knowledge, pride, and one of the more infamous kings in Jewish history. The similarities of Daniel 4 to the Nabonidus literature do not function as allusion (i.e., the reader is not expected to know the Nabonidus stories in order to fully appreciate Daniel 4), but rather, the similarities function to *displace* the Nabonidus material (cf. Lacocque, 75), much in the same way that David's slaying of Goliath attempts (1 Samuel 17) to displace Elhanan's slaying of the giant (2 Sam 21:19).

[13]In terms of form, he connects character dialogue, bits of straight narration, and doxologies. In terms of content, he associates pieces of the story which have the same vocabulary, the same subject matter, and similar actions.

[14]Chatman (233) writes:

> In "unreliable narration" the narrator's account is at odds with the implied reader's surmises about the story's real intentions. The story undermines the discourse. We conclude, by "reading out," between the lines, that the events and existents could not have been "like that," and so we hold the narrator suspect . . . . The implied author has established a secret communication with the implied reader.

See also Booth, 304-309, 432.

Because the character-narrator is built around the reputation of a historical personage, the effect of the story is dependent upon an unspoken familiarity with history on both the parts of the third-person narrator and the implied external audience. The historical Nebuchadnezzar was never a convert to Israelite religion. If he worshiped a "Most High," he certainly did not identify the deity with the god of the Jews. If we as readers know this, then what are we to make of this testimony? The reader may face the same situation in the book of Jonah, where the story describes the conversion and subsequent sparing of Nineveh, but the reader may know that Nineveh, as well as Jonah's precious Jerusalem temple, is eventually destroyed. In light of this information, how then does the reader interpret the role of God in the story of Jonah?

[15]The irony of re-membering history parallels yet another dimension of the dream in Daniel 2: In a diachronic reading of the dream, the great image represents a chronological sequence of kings or kingdoms. The stone destroys all simultaneously—the "first" are destroyed with the "last" as if in attempt to exorcise a part of history that still troubled later readers. Here in Daniel 4 this part of history is not exorcised but substantially revised.

Notes to Chapter Five: Your Father the King

[1]We need not rely on historical information for this understanding, though historical information does support this. We need only read the introduction to the book in 1:1-2, Daniel's interpretations of Nebuchadnezzar's dreams in chapters 2 and 4, and Nebuchadnezzar's own words in 4:30 to see that the narrator has portrayed Nebuchadnezzar from the beginning as a king of great accomplishment. This will be further supported by Daniel's speech later in chapter 5.

[2]Indeed, the character Belshazzar son of Nebuchadnezzar stands in a tradition of weak sons of strong fathers, for example, the sons of Eli, the sons of Samuel, the son of Solomon.

[3]There were, after all, supposedly no divine images in the Jerusalem

temple. From a pagan point of view, the vessels might be considered substitutive.

[4]The narrator expects the implied reader, a reader with a knowledge of and an investment in the larger story of Israel, to have an interest in the temple vessels (see 1:2).

[5]The question here is one of motivation. Although Belshazzar's action is later interpreted by Daniel (and implicitly so by God, the narrator, and probably the reader) to be a direct affront to the lord of heaven, we are not justified in assuming that this is what Belshazzar intends. Nothing in the text so far suggests that he is attempting to challenge directly the god of Jerusalem or the god of heaven. If that were his intention, then he should not be surprised at the divine response. We have already seen other examples of the difference between a character's intention and how God, the narrator and probably the reader interprets the character's action or speech. In chapter 3 Nebuchadnezzar asks Shadrach, Meshach, and Abednego, "Who is the god who will deliver you from my hands?" (vs. 15). His intention is to challenge the three men who stand before him, but, in actuality his question challenges the god whom they serve. Likewise, in chapter 4, when Nebuchadnezzar stands surveying Babylon and praises himself (vs. 30 [27]), he never intends to offend any deity. Nevertheless, the God of heaven interprets the comment to be offensive.

[6]This depiction of the fate of the temple vessels represents a theme of hope for and restoration of the exiles and their way of life. So, too, with other traditions concerning the vessels' capture (e.g., 2 Chron 36:7, 18; Ezra 1:7-11; Isa 52:11; Jer 27:19-22) rather than their complete destruction (i.e., melting them down for their elementary materials, as in 2 Kgs 24:13; 25:13-17)—see Ackroyd. Like the ark of the Lord housed in the temple of Dagon (1 Samuel 5)—to the Philistines a symbol of their victory, but in fact a cloaked, divine power—the vessels represent to Nebuchadnezzar the defeat of the god of Jerusalem, but to the reader they represent Adonai's presence and ultimate victory.

[7]In this sense, Lacocque's intuition concerning Belshazzar is on target: Belshazzar is, indeed, as Lacocque suggests, trying to reassure himself by degrading what intimidates him. However, what intimidates him, I would argue, is not the god of Jerusalem *per se*, but the reputation of his father.

[8]One might also read this episode in a less Freudian vein as Belshazzar's attempt to assume some of Nebuchadnezzar's power and prestige by associating himself with the objects of his father's victory.

[9]Belshazzar sends for the vessels *bitem hamra*ʾ, "when he tasted the wine" or "under the influence [literally: decree] of the wine." The phrase is ambiguous.

[10]Shea (1985b) has pointed to the Nabonidus Chronicle (ANET, 306) as evidence that this list of gods in Daniel 5 reflects an historical occurrence. According to the Chronicle, Nabonidus, in the last year of his reign, gathered numerous gods from other cities and transported them to Babylon, supposedly

for the purpose of reinforcing the city's defenses. Based upon the Chronicle and excavational evidence at Babylon, Shea (306-307) states, ". . . there was no shortage of gods for Belshazzar and his friends to praise . . . for a considerable number of gods had been added to those normally present in the city." Shea's observations are helpful in that they point out that, in the ancient world, the stockpiling of gods could be equated with the stockpiling of power, an idea which is at work in the story of Daniel 5. The list in the context of chapter 5 suggests that, for Belshazzar, more gods mean more favor, more success, more power. On the other hand, whatever the historical evidence, the information provided by the story takes precedence when we are interpreting the *story* rather than reconstructing the history of Babylon. The story character Belshazzar expresses no concern for the defense of the city. The story does not mention that the gods are new to Babylon. Perhaps the storyteller does borrow a historical motif, but rather than attempting to describe accurately what went on in Babylon on the eve of its destruction, the storyteller uses the list of deities as a reflection of Belshazzar's personal ambition.

[11]Beginning with Josephus, most commentators on this text have agreed that the queen here is the queen mother. The story world supports this identification. The narrator has told us that the wives and concubines of Belshazzar are already present. The queen speaks to him with familiarity and a certain degree of authority. Furthermore, the queen's knowledge of Nebuchadnezzar and his reign indicates that she is more likely the wife or mother of Nebuchadnezzar than the wife of Belshazzar.

[12]Most English translations leave out the final phrase, "your father the king," though it has good textual support.

[13]The similarity in the names of the sage and king is striking. Both, we assume, reflect the name of Nebuchadnezzar's god. Is the queen taunting the king with the suggestion that, since Nebuchadnezzar gave his sage and his son almost identical names, he thought as much of this sage as he did of his son?

[14]I disagree, however, with Lacocque's interpretation (101) that Belshazzar's promise of reward is an "attempt to bribe the 'divine' and to change a 'fate.' "

[15]Quoting Heaton, 160; Towner 1984:74; Porteous, 80. Most commentators have discussed the sternness of Daniel's response. Heaton (160) indicates that the tone of Daniel's reply is surprising and stands in direct contrast to Daniel's earlier attitude toward Nebuchadnezzar in chapter 4. Porteous (80-81) admits that Daniel's refusal of reward is out of character and rather limply suggests that the refusal might be intended as a lesson to Jewish sages concerning their dealings with foreign rulers. See also Anderson, 59. Some scholars have expressed no surprise at the tone of Daniel's response; they have, nevertheless, attempted to justify Daniel's rudeness by magnifying Belshazzar's transgression (e.g., Lacocque, Hartman and DiLella).

[16]Nebuchadnezzar's strength is paralleled to God's in that, just as God

raises and lowers "whomever he pleases," so does Nebuchadnezzar.

[17]That is to say that the meaning of the writing on the wall lies not in any mysterious historical referents (cf. Ginsberg, Kraeling, Freedman) but in the context of the story itself.

[18]Playing upon words and embellishing texts seems to have been acceptable in the ancient Jewish practice of *pesher* or interpretation. The clue to interpretation is often the double meaning of a word. See Finkel, 360; Fishbane; Silberman.

[19]Lacocque's reading (95)—that, because of Belshazzar's act, "the Spirit is dislodged from the vases where it was hiding . . . then openly reveals itself on the whitewashed wall from whence it can never again be erased"—is picturesque but does not account for the severe judgment that falls upon the king.

[20]Daniel's reading and interpreting the words on the wall exemplifies the reading process itself: It is impossible to read with complete objectivity, without passing judgment, without becoming personally involved.

[21]Some have suggested that the folktale plot requires that the successful sage must receive his reward (Hartman and DiLella, 190). Yet this part of the plot is quite expendable, as we have seen in chapter 4. And in any case, even if material is included to conform the narrative to a conventional plot, it still has its effect upon how one reads character. This is another case where an appeal to the mechanics of composition does not dispose of the question of what the text means. Cf. above on the question of why the queen introduces Daniel as if he were unknown to Belshazzar.

[22]And so security and presumption are issues that challenge the reader, the one interpreting, the one passing judgment upon the text. Do we, like the queen, think that once the interpretation is given, the meaning, and thus the problem, of the text is solved?

Notes to Chapter Six: All the King's Men

[1]The odd word (*rgš*) describing the assembly of these men has an indeterminable meaning that ranges from the rather innocent connotation of "in company" to the idea of "conspiracy" to the notion of "rage" (see Montgomery, 272-73). All of these nuances are at play in the context of the present story. The ministers and officials obviously assemble themselves before the king. They are, as we know from verses 5-6, conspiring against Daniel. Considering that there are 122 of them, it seems unlikely that they could gather together without causing a certain amount of disturbance!

[2]When considering the king's reasons for approving the measure one could argue that the proposal of ultimate sovereignty appeals to Darius's ego

(cf. Towner 1984:81-82): this a man wanting to be a god. The thirty day limitation, however, rather undercuts this desire as a possible motivation. Besides, the wording of the edict, "to make a petition" or "to make a request," is ambiguous. It may, but does not necessarily, specify the *worship* of Darius. If the edict appeals to the king's ego (which, to some extent, it must), I would suggest that it is more likely because he interprets both the proposal and the crowd before him as indicating his subjects' overwhelming support.

[3]The RSV/NRSV translation "I have done no wrong" (6:22 [23]) unfortunately misses the word play and, in the context, suggests Daniel to be lying. "Wrong" is relative. Daniel has defied the king's edict and has, according to the law, done "wrong." However, in doing "wrong," Daniel has done nothing *harmful*. Just as the officials wanted the king to think that Daniel's defiance of the edict was injurious to the king himself, Daniel is saying that his defiance of the edict has nothing to do with his loyalty to the king.

[4]The translation "he was faithful to [or in the matter of]" (6:23 [24]) is more appropriate than the RSV/NRSV, "he had trusted in," because the latter not only suggests passive belief, but also implies that Daniel is saved because he trusts in God's deliverance. The story clearly shows Daniel's faithfulness to be active. It is, according to the narrator, because of his active loyalty to God that God is actively loyal to him. The story is not so much dealing with "trust in" as "fidelity to" both god and king.

[5]This same motif of "overkill" and the shadows that it casts on the characters involved can also be found in chapters 8 and 9 of Esther. The Esther narrative raises the question, When does defense become offense? Daniel 6 raises the question, When does punishment for wrongdoing become personal revenge?

[6]On the reconstitution of society as a comic device, see Good, 55.

[7]In other words, the motif of the "irrevocable law of the Medes and Persians" contributes, as it does in the book of Esther, to the tension of the plot. The conflict produced by the irrevocable law, however, is a false construct. The reader cannot know this for sure until the end of the story, although Darius's struggle to rescue Daniel hints that this is the case. Consequently, Darius's decree at the end signals that the reader should back up and reinterpret what actually is at stake in the preceding situation.

[8]Compare the indictment of a certain king in Daniel 7, that he seeks "to change the times and the *law*" (vs. 25).

[9]Gunn (1984:128) expresses it this way:

> [The book] makes clear that to choose Yahweh, to "fear" Yahweh, to respond to Yahweh in faith, comes only by divine decree or out of human freedom. It cannot come by human decree. No one can secure God (it is a familar theme!). The book is punctuated by decrees. The injunction to 'worship the image' in chapter 3 gives place to 'fear before the God of Daniel' in chapter 6. Against the irony of the king

decreeing the worship of Yahweh (Daniel's god!) is set the irony of his unawareness that such is not his to decree. In humility he still plays God! Here is but the obverse of the tyrant who decrees worship of *other* gods. Both decrees are ultimately absurd. The irony, therefore, touches *all* who think to enforce religion—it is a message to Constantine, as it is to Antiochus.

Notes to Chapter Seven: Envisioning Sovereignty

[1]The word *ngʿ* can mean "strike" as well as "touch" (RSV). "Strike" seems to make more sense in the context of bringing someone out of a catatonic state.

[2]Tradition testifies to the uneasy placement of this hymn. The tradition reflected in the Masoretic text places the doxology at the end of chapter 3. Greek translators moved the material to the end of chapter 4 alongside vss. 34-35. Theodotion-Daniel moved the hymn back to its present place in the Aramaic text. Most modern English versions place the material at the beginning of chapter 4 because of the introductory nature of the formula and its consistency with the first person account that follows. On the different versions of Daniel, see Hartman and DiLella, 72-84, and Montgomery, 24-57.

[3]Read in the context of chapter 3, moreover, it forms part of a larger section, 3:29-4:3 [3:29-33], which shares the same elements (though not in the same order) as are found in 6:25-28 [26-29]: There is a decree concerning worship, a notice that the heroes prosper, and a doxology.

[4]Note that the attitude here toward Cyrus is vastly different from that expressed in Isaiah 40-55.

[5]Despite the fact that the third-person narrator in 10:1 wants us to believe that Daniel understands the final vision, Daniel himself admits that he does not (12:8).

[6]This is, of course, why various people throughout history have understood these visions to be referring to their own situation. See, for example, Towner's discussion (1983) of whether the English Puritans were 'the Saints of the Most High.' "

[7]Gunn (1984:123), in stressing the importance of the Babylonian king's expanding knowledge of God, draws attention to the similarity with Pharaoh in Exodus 1-14. Gunn's line of thought on the theological significance (and irony) of divine recognition has been germinal for this present reading of Daniel. See, for example, his comment (1982:83-84; cf. 89):

> It is not only Egypt and the nations who will learn of God's power. . . . Yahweh's demonstration of his power over the Egyptians is also

bound up with his need to establish himself securely as Israel's God, the god of the covenantal promise, in the eyes of Israel . . . . After all, what does it profit God if he 'provides' but his people fail to identify their provider? It is a vulnerability of all gods! Yahweh needs Israel, just as Israel needs Yahweh. Thus by his signs and wonders Yahweh seeks to secure his identity.

[8]The issue is being discussed in terms of epistemology—the knowledge of God. Why is recognition so important to God? Why is God so determined to gain the recognition of these kings? Can it be that epistomology casts a shadow on ontology,—that God is not sovereign until God is recognized as sovereign?

[9]The determinism that scholars have long recognized as characteristic of apocalyptic ideology, then, can be read in Daniel as an attempt to answer the irony of divine and human sovereignty that emerges from Daniel. Cf. Gunn 1984:127-128.

[10]The connection between lions and monarchs is playfully alluded to in the language used in 6:24, literally, "the lions ruled over them."

BIBLIOGRAPHY

Ackroyd, Peter. 1972. "The Temple Vessels—A Continuity Theme." *Vetus Testamentum Supplements* 23:166-81.

Alter, Robert. 1981. *The Art of Biblical Narrative.* New York: Basic Books.

Anderson, Robert A. 1984. *Signs and Wonders: A Commentary on the Book of Daniel.* Grand Rapids: Eerdmans.

Baldwin, Joyce. 1978. *Daniel.* Downers Grove, Illinois: Intervarsity.

Bar-Efrat, Shimon. 1989. *Narrative Art in the Bible.* Translated by Dorothea Shefer-Vanson. Sheffield: Almond.

Bentzen, Aage. 1937. *Daniel.* Tübingen: J. C. B. Mohr.

Berlin, Adele. 1983. *Poetics and Interpretation of Biblical Narrative.* Sheffield: Almond, 1983.

Booth, Wayne C. 1961. *The Rhetoric of Fiction.* Chicago: University of Chicago.

Brown, Robert McAfee. 1984. "Furnaces and Faith: 'But If Not. . . .' " In *Unexpected News: Reading the Bible With Third World Eyes,* 142-56. Philadelphia: Westminster.

Campbell, Joseph. 1949. *A Hero with a Thousand Faces.* Princeton: Princeton University.

Chatman, Seymour. 1978. *Story and Discourse: Narrative Structure in Fiction and Film.* Ithaca: Cornell.

Collins, John J. 1977. *The Apocalyptic Vision of the Book of Daniel.* Missoula: Scholars.

——. 1981. *Daniel, First Maccabees, Second Maccabees.* Wilmington, Delaware: Michael Glazier.

——. 1984. *Daniel with an Introduction to Apocalyptic Literature.* FOTL 20. Grand Rapids: Eerdmans.

Coxon, Peter W. 1976. "Daniel 3:17: A Linguistic and Theological Problem." *Vetus Testamentum* 26:400-405.

——. 1986. "The Great Tree of Daniel 4." In *A Word in Season: Essays in Honor of William McKane,* 91-111. Edited by J. D. Martin and P. R. Davies. Sheffield: JSOT, 1986.

Davies, Philip R. 1976. "Daniel Chapter Two." *Journal of Theological Studies* 27:392-401.

——. 1985. *Daniel.* Sheffield: JSOT.

Daly, Mary. 1973. *Beyond God the Father*. Boston: Beacon.

DiLella, Alexander. 1981. "Daniel 4:7-14: Poetic Analysis and Biblical Background." In *Mélanges bibliques et orientaux en l'honneur de M. Henri Cazelles*, 247-58. Edited by A. Caquot and M. Delcor. Neukirchen-Vluyn: Neukirchener.

Driver, S. R. 1905. *The Book of Daniel*. Cambridge: Cambridge University.

Dupont-Sommer, A. 1961. *The Essene Writings from Qumran*. Translated by G. Vermes. Cleveland: World.

Finkel, A. 1963. "The Pesher of Dreams and Scriptures." *Revue de Qumran* 4:357-370.

Fishbane, Michael. 1977. "The Qumran Pesher and Traits of Ancient Hermeneutics." *Proceedings of the Sixth World Congress of Jewish Studies* 1:97-114.

Flusser, D. 1972. "The Four Empires in the Fourth Sibyl and in the Book of Daniel." *Israel Oriental Studies* 2:148-75.

Freedman, David Noel. 1957. "The Prayer of Nabonidus." *Bulletin of the American Schools of Oriental Research* 145:31-32.

Genette, Gerard. 1980. *Narrative Discourse: An Essay in Method*.Translated by J. E. Lewin. Ithaca: Cornell University.

Gennep, Arnold van. 1960. *Rites of Passage*. Chicago: University of Chicago.

Ginsberg, H. L. 1948. *Studies in Daniel*. New York: Jewish Theological Seminary of America.

——. 1954. "The Composition of the Book of Daniel." *Vetus Testamentum* 4:246-75.

Good, Edwin. 1984. "Apocalyptic as Comedy: The Book of Daniel." *Semeia* 32:41-70.

Gowan, Donald. 1975. *When Man Becomes God: Humanism and Hybris in the Old Testament*. Pittsburgh: Pickwick.

Gunn, David M. 1982. "The 'Hardening of Pharaoh's Heart': Plot, Character and Theology in Exodus 1-14." In *Art and Meaning: Rhetoric in Biblical Literature*, 72-96. Edited by D. J. A. Clines, D. M. Gunn, and A. J. Hauser. Sheffield: JSOT.

——. 1984. "The Anatomy of Divine Comedy: On Reading the Bible as Comedy and Tragedy." *Semeia* 32:115-129.

Gunn, David M. and Danna Nolan Fewell. 1992. *Narrative in the Hebrew Bible*. Oxford and New York: Oxford University.

Hartman, Louis. 1962. "The Great Tree and Nabuchodonosor's Madness." In *The Bible in Current Catholic Thought*, 75-82. Edited by John L. McKenzie. New York: Herder and Herder.

Hartman, Louis and Alexander A. DiLella. 1978. *The Book of Daniel*. Garden City, New York: Doubleday.

Hasel, G. F. 1956. "The Four World Empires of Daniel 2 Against Its Near Eastern Environment." *Journal for the Study of the Old Testament* 12:17-30.

Heaton, E. W. 1956. *The Book of Daniel*. London: SCM.

Humphreys, W. Lee. 1973. "A Life-Style for Diaspora: A Study of the Tales of Esther and Daniel." *Journal of Biblical Literature* 92:211-23.

Johnson, Barbara. 1986. "The Critical Difference: BartheS/BalZac." In *Contemporary Literary Criticism*, 439-46. Edited by Robert Con Davis. New York, London: Longman.

Knight, G. A. F. 1971. "The Book of Daniel." In *The Interpreter's One-Volume Commentary on the Bible*, 436-50. Edited by C. M. Laymon. Nashville: Abingdon.

Kraeling, E. G. H. 1944. "The Handwriting on the Wall." *Journal of Biblical Literature* 63:11-18.

Kuhl, Curt. 1930. *Die drei Männer im Feuer*. Giessen: Töpelmann.

Lacocque, André. 1979. *The Book of Daniel*. Translated by David Pellauer. Atlanta: John Knox.

McNutt, Paula. 1990. *The Forging of Israel: Iron Technology, Symbolism and Tradition in Ancient Society*. Sheffield: Almond.

Milne, Pamela J. 1988. *Vladimir Propp and the Study of Structure in Hebrew Biblical Narrative*. Sheffield: Almond.

Miscall, Peter D. 1983. *The Workings of Old Testament Narrative*. Philadelphia: Fortress/Chico, California: Scholars.

Montgomery, J. A. 1927. *The Book of Daniel*. Edinburgh: T. & T. Clark.

Niditch, Susan and Robert Doran. 1977. "The Success Story of the Wise Courtier: A Formal Approach." *Journal of Biblical Literature* 96:179-93.

Plöger, Otto. 1965. *Das Buch Daniel*. Gutersloh: Gutersloher, Gerd Mohn.

Porteous, Norman. 1965. *Daniel*. London: SCM.

Rabinowitz, Peter J. 1980. "'What's Hecuba to Us?' The Audience's Experience of Literary Borrowing." In *The Reader in the Text: Essays on Audience and Interpretation*, 241-63. Edited by Susan R. Suleiman and Inge Crosman. Princeton: Princeton University.

Shea, William. 1982. "Daniel 3: Extra-Biblical Texts and the Convocation on the Plain of Dura." *Andrews University Seminary Studies* 20:29-52.

——. 1985a. "Further Literary Structures in Daniel 2-7: An Analysis of Daniel 4." *Andrews University Seminary Studies* 23:193-202.

——. 1985b. "Further Literary Structures in Daniel 2-7: An Analysis of Daniel 5, and the Broader Relationships within Chapters 2-7." *Andrews University Seminary Studies* 23:277-95.

Siegmann, E. F. 1956. "The Stone Hewn from the Mountain." *Catholic Biblical Quarterly* 18:364-79.

Silberman, L. H. 1961. "Unriddling the Riddle: A Study in the Structure and Language of the Habakkuk Pesher." *Revue de Qumran* 3:323-64.

Silverman, Kaja. 1983. *The Subject of Semiotics*. Oxford: Oxford University.

Slotki, Judah. 1951. *Daniel, Ezra, and Nehemiah*. London: Soncino.

Sternberg, Meir. 1985. *The Poetics of Biblical Narrative: Ideological Literature and the Drama of Reading*. Bloomington: Indiana University.

Towner, W. Sibley. 1969. "Poetic Passages of Daniel 1-6." *Catholic Biblical Quarterly* 31:317-26.
——. 1984. *Daniel*. Atlanta: John Knox.
Turner, Victor. 1967. *The Forest of Symbols*. Ithaca: Cornell University.
——. 1969. *The Ritual Process*. Chicago: Aldine.
——. 1974. *Dramas, Fields, and Metaphors*. Ithaca: Cornell University.
Uspensky, Boris. 1973. *A Poetics of Composition: The Structure of the Artistic Text and Typology of a Compositional Form*. Translated by Valentina Zavarin and Susan Wittig. Berkeley: University of California.
Wharton, James. 1985. "Daniel 3:16-18." *Interpretation* 39:170-6.

INDEXES

Authors

Biblical and Other Ancient References

(continued)